Serving Under Ruperra
1900 – 1939

Serving Under Ruperra
1900 – 1939

by Pat Moseley

Printed by Clarke Printing, Monmouth

Published by Pat Jones-Jenkins

Copyright © Pat Moseley

ISBN 978-0-9561464-1-0

SERVING UNDER RUPERRA
1900 – 1939

Compiled by Pat Moseley and the members of Rudry Local History Group from conversations with local people, and their friends and relations in the 1980s and 90s and from material donated by them.

Dedications and credits.

This book is dedicated to all the people who believe in the importance of their heritage and who have shown interest in and encouraged me in the production of this book.

It is also dedicated to those who have helped me, nearer to the work face and bravely endured the compiling of the finished product.

Photographs and prints are credited in italics in the general index. Those not credited are either in the public domain or taken by the author.

This book is partly funded by Cadw's 'Civic Initiative (Heritage) Grant Scheme' which aims to increase awareness of the built heritage of Wales and promote its appreciation.
Printed by Clarke Printing, Monmouth
Cover Design and other graphics by Chris Jones-Jenkins
Copyright: Pat Moseley

For further information about the work of the Ruperra Trusts visit the Websites: www.ruperra.org.uk and www.ruperracastle.blogspot.com

SERVING UNDER RUPERRA
1900 – 1939

CONTENTS	PAGE
Introduction and Acknowledgements	1
Chronological Table and Sale Map of 1935	4
Map of places in the Book	6
Chapter One A Castle fit for a King	8
Chapter Two Was Life Better One Hundred Years Ago?	14
Chapter Three Estate Houses and their Occupants	22
Chapter Four An Introduction to the 20th Century	36
Chapter Five Running the Estate	46
Chapter Six Angus and Agnes McKinnon	64
Chapter Seven A Little Girl's Story	81
Chapter Eight Coed Craig Ruperra, the Ancient Woodland	86
Chapter Nine Housework in the Castle and Estate.	94
Chapter Ten Impressions of the Castle	106
Chapter Eleven The End of the Estate	113
Further Reading	117
Glossary of Welsh Place Names	119
Index	120

INTRODUCTION AND ACKNOWLEDGEMENTS

The printing of this book has been partly funded by Cadw's Civic Initiative (Heritage) Grant Scheme. This aims to help local people to become acquainted with and to appreciate their heritage. Many of those mentioned in the book are and were already very involved with their heritage and I hope that together we will interest the remaining ones. It is widely recognised that we all need to know where we come from and that we receive energy from the past. As with plants, survival without roots is difficult and likewise, our roots are very localised. Yet modern day facilities link us not only to the heritage roots of our own country but to those of all the world's peoples. In this way, we can all move on into the future with mutual understanding.

Compiling other people's memories is such a pleasurable task. Vivid visual images are evoked and although we know that these happenings were real, we also know that they are gone, that we cannot bring them back but can only look at them as through a net curtain while we try to share in them. Yet, as we listen, we realise that these happenings were as magical to the people who experienced them as they are to us; they love talking about them; they are describing things that are very dear to them. Their stories are almost like the legends of another age, which used to be handed down the generations without ever being written down. A social evening even as near as a hundred years ago in many parts of the country, was a gathering of people to listen to stories of the past. Nowadays we can read them, listen to them on radio, watch them on television, and at any time we choose. Yet even today the recording must continue because in another hundred years' time, people's lives will have changed so much again.

Rather than an accurate description of life on the Ruperra Estate in the early 20th century, this book will portray how people thought and felt about this life, how they perceived their neighbours, their own families, their surroundings as well as their lords and masters who provided their means of living. There is a great deal more research needed to be done about this period of our local heritage at Ruperra. Now that some of the memories have been preserved, I hope that somebody after me will take on that research. There are boxes of Tredegar papers waiting in the National

Library of Wales to be researched and there is something on almost every page of this book that could support more thorough research.

The boundary and condition of the old Ruperra Estate is still almost the same as it was a hundred years ago. Wholesale development has not yet happened and it is easy to visualise the 'old days.' The road from Risca to Lower Machen over Ochrwyth is the way the poachers used to come to Ruperra from Risca. On an evening walk along the Ruperra Drive from the Rudry Road to Ruperra Castle the ruins of some of the four Parkwall cottages can still be seen. They once echoed with the sounds of children playing and their mothers calling them in, with the noise of the rumbling, creaking wheels of the Morgan family's coaches and the galloping horses, and later the new motorised transport, going to Tredegar House perhaps, or to the Houses of Parliament in London or just coming home to Ruperra Castle in the evening.

We can imagine the estate workers treading the paths leading to the Castle, clambering over steps in the now crumbling estate walls to start their daily tasks. Two thousand years ago tribes and chieftains trod the paths to Coed Craig Ruperra, gathering for special ceremonies. Today, many people empathise with those who went before them, who saw the same mountains and valleys and the same beautiful countryside. Some even wonder what would have been their role in a previous age – a slave or a chieftain, a head gardener or a hedge trimmer, a lord or a servant. It is these people who have made this book possible.

The original members of Rudry Local History Group worked hard recording the details of the Tithe Schedules and Census returns for Rudry and Michaelstone y Fedw, which together with the tape recordings, provided the information for this book. So many kind and interested people lent or gave photographs, documents, out of print books and newspaper articles and willingly recorded their own memories and those of their friends and forebears.

For the chapter on Angus McKinnon, I am indebted to his grandsons, Ian and Angus, and to Peter Kerr, who hopes he is related! Also Kathy Renouf and through her Kathleen M. Burgess of the Surrey Gardens Trust. For the chapter on William Beechey, I am grateful to the late Herbie Spring for lending me the diary and also to Elwyn Edwards, the grandson of William Beechey.

There are obviously too many to name but this book is a tribute to all people who care about their heritage and about beautiful historic countryside. They know that knowledge and appreciation of the past can inspire and enhance the quality of their lives and those of their future descendants.

Chronological Table

The Ruperra Estate from the 17th century on was part of the vast Tredegar Estates owned by the Morgans of Tredegar. From the mid 19th century the Lord Tredegar of the time would possibly have spent his childhood at Ruperra Castle, moving on to Tredegar House when he inherited the title but always having great affection for Ruperra. When the servants talk about 'Lord Tredegar' it could have been Colonel Godfrey, Commander Courtenay, Evan or John, but it doesn't really matter; we don't need to be exact about their lordships' visits to Ruperra. In any case like all aristocratic landowners they spent a good deal of time away, staying at their other properties. In the late 19th and early 20th centuries, Godfrey and then Courtenay sat in the House of Lords while Colonel Freddie was MP for Monmouthshire. Indeed according to the sales particulars for Ruperra in 1935, London was only two and a half hours away by non-stop express train. They also spent time shooting and hunting on other landowners' estates. The servants meanwhile kept the home fires burning.

1854 The Charge of the Light Brigade. Both Godfrey and Frederick, (Freddie) sons of Sir Charles Morgan Robinson Morgan (1792- 1875, created first Baron Tredegar in 1859), served in the Crimean War.
1875 Godfrey became Lord Tredegar and moved from Ruperra to Tredegar House. Colonel Freddie, his brother, continued to live at Ruperra.
1894 Angus McKinnon became Head Gardener at Ruperra.
1895 Fire destroyed the Stable Block at Ruperra.
1899 William Beechey at Home Farm Ruperra made his first diary entries.
1901 Queen Victoria died.
1905 Godfrey was created Viscount Tredegar
1906 Bert Stradling started work at Ruperra. The earliest audio memories.
1908 The new stable block was finished.
1909 The unexpected death of Colonel Freddie. His son Courtenay continued the refurbishment of Ruperra .
1913 On the death of Godfrey, Courtenay became Lord Tredegar
1913 The famous glass house was built by Mackenzie and Moncur Ltd.
1922 Mary Thomas started work in the Bothy
1926 Courtenay was created Viscount Tredegar.
1934 Evan Morgan, son of Courtenay, became Lord Tredegar.
1935 A sale of the contents of the Castle followed the failure to sell Ruperra.
1949 John Morgan, Evan's cousin became Lord Tredegar and last Baron.
1956/7 The Tredegar Estates including Ruperra were sold.
1962 John died. The end of the Morgan line.

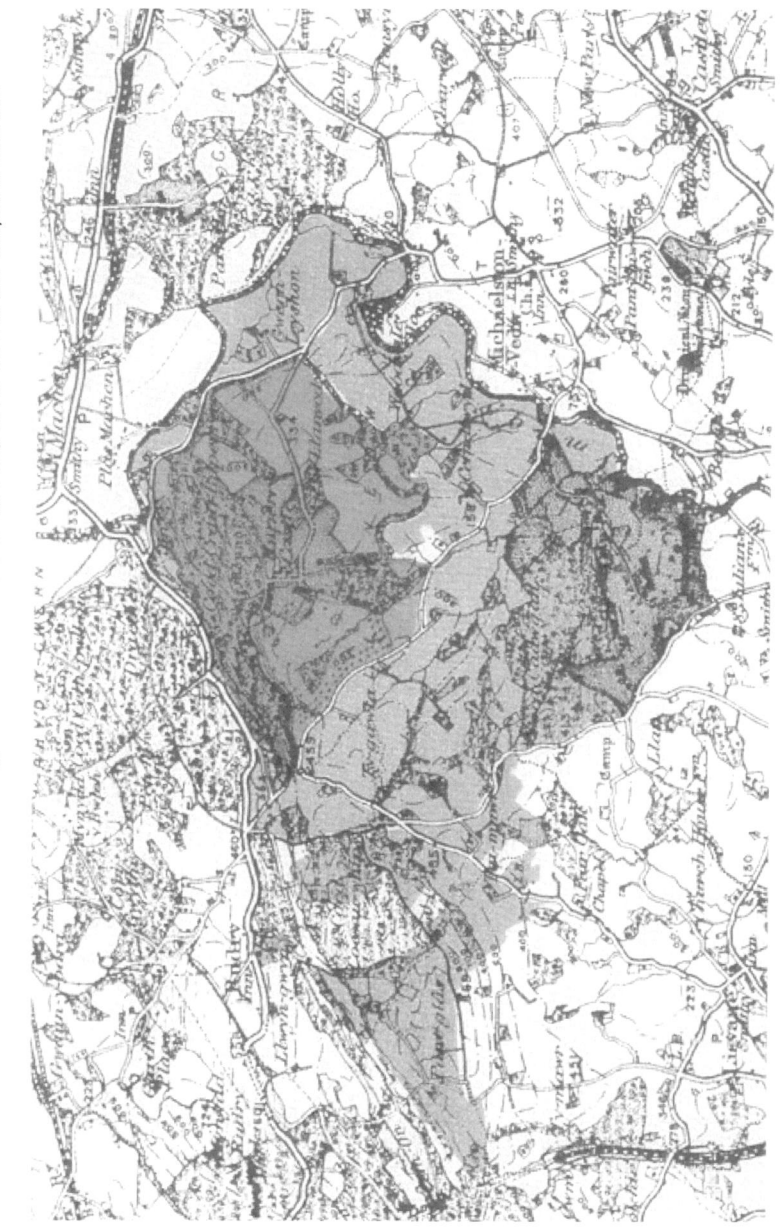

The Sale Map of the Ruperra Estate in 1935 showing the smaller area of 870 acres (dark area at the top) and the larger area of 3,140 acres. It was advertised as "The Historic, Agricultural and Sporting Estate" There were no offers. At the time of the final sale in the 1950s the whole of the Tredegar Estates including Ruperra covered 53,000 acres.

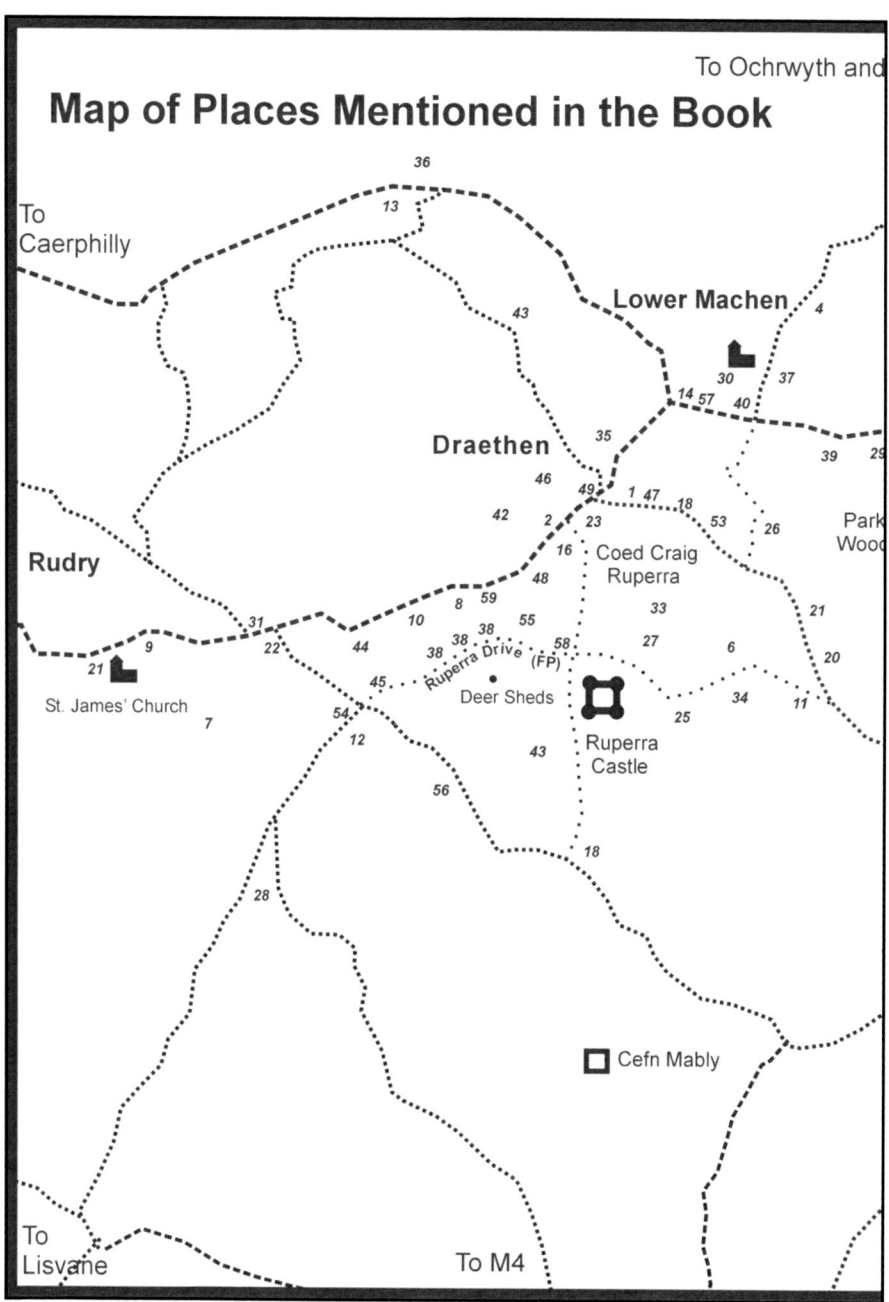

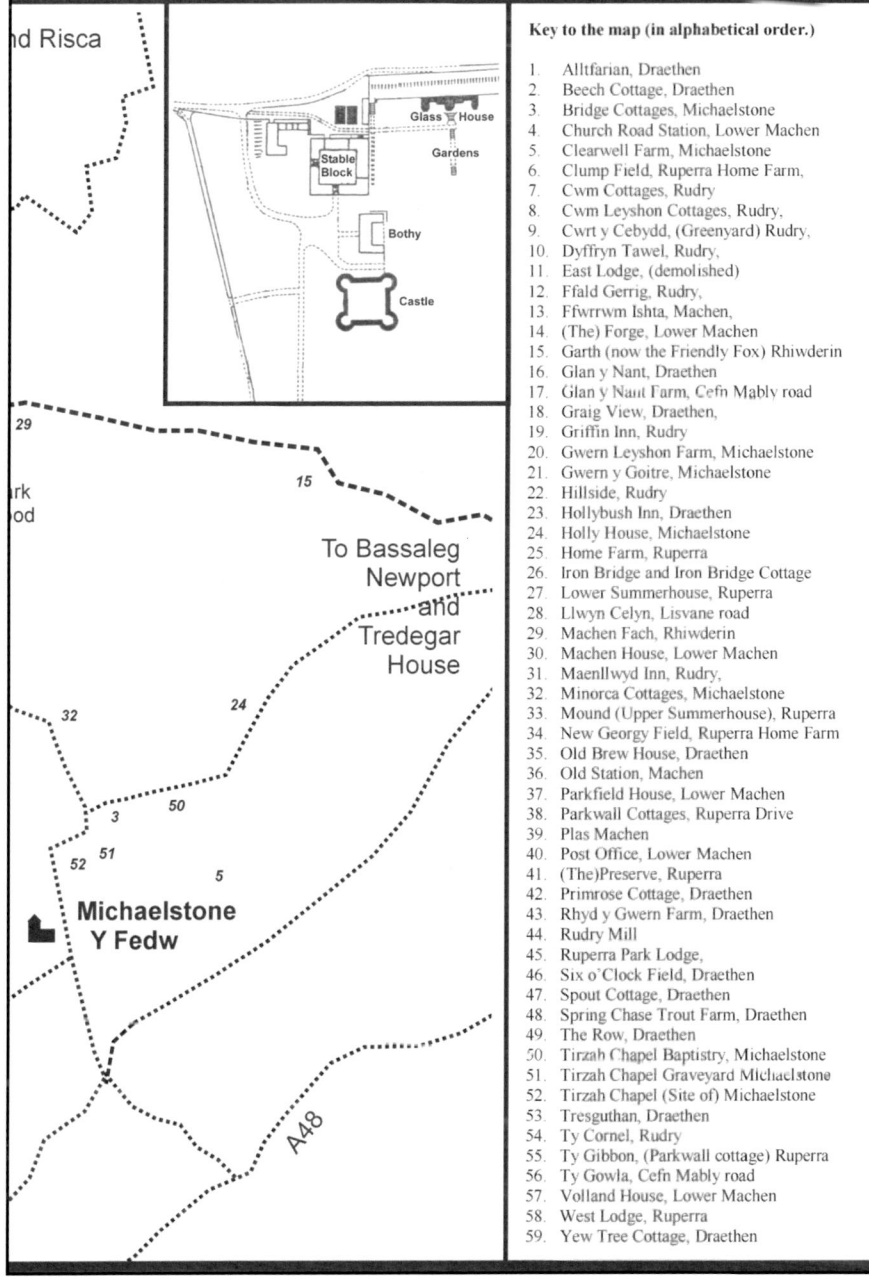

Key to the map (in alphabetical order.)

1. Alltfarian, Draethen
2. Beech Cottage, Draethen
3. Bridge Cottages, Michaelstone
4. Church Road Station, Lower Machen
5. Clearwell Farm, Michaelstone
6. Clump Field, Ruperra Home Farm,
7. Cwm Cottages, Rudry
8. Cwm Leyshon Cottages, Rudry,
9. Cwrt y Cebydd, (Greenyard) Rudry,
10. Dyffryn Tawel, Rudry,
11. East Lodge, (demolished)
12. Ffald Gerrig, Rudry,
13. Ffwrrwm Ishta, Machen,
14. (The) Forge, Lower Machen
15. Garth (now the Friendly Fox) Rhiwderin
16. Glan y Nant, Draethen
17. Glan y Nant Farm, Cefn Mably road
18. Graig View, Draethen,
19. Griffin Inn, Rudry
20. Gwern Leyshon Farm, Michaelstone
21. Gwern y Goitre, Michaelstone
22. Hillside, Rudry
23. Hollybush Inn, Draethen
24. Holly House, Michaelstone
25. Home Farm, Ruperra
26. Iron Bridge and Iron Bridge Cottage
27. Lower Summerhouse, Ruperra
28. Llwyn Celyn, Lisvane road
29. Machen Fach, Rhiwderin
30. Machen House, Lower Machen
31. Maenllwyd Inn, Rudry,
32. Minorca Cottages, Michaelstone
33. Mound (Upper Summerhouse), Ruperra
34. New Georgy Field, Ruperra Home Farm
35. Old Brew House, Draethen
36. Old Station, Machen
37. Parkfield House, Lower Machen
38. Parkwall Cottages, Ruperra Drive
39. Plas Machen
40. Post Office, Lower Machen
41. (The)Preserve, Ruperra
42. Primrose Cottage, Draethen
43. Rhyd y Gwern Farm, Draethen
44. Rudry Mill
45. Ruperra Park Lodge,
46. Six o'Clock Field, Draethen
47. Spout Cottage, Draethen
48. Spring Chase Trout Farm, Draethen
49. The Row, Draethen
50. Tirzah Chapel Baptistry, Michaelstone
51. Tirzah Chapel Graveyard Michaelstone
52. Tirzah Chapel (Site of) Michaelstone
53. Tresguthan, Draethen
54. Ty Cornel, Rudry
55. Ty Gibbon, (Parkwall cottage) Ruperra
56. Ty Gowla, Cefn Mably road
57. Volland House, Lower Machen
58. West Lodge, Ruperra
59. Yew Tree Cottage, Draethen

CHAPTER ONE A CASTLE FIT FOR A KING.

Ruperra lies in a triangle of relatively unspoilt, open rolling countryside between the rapidly expanding conurbations of Cardiff, Newport and Caerphilly. Once part of the 53,000 acre Tredegar Estates, which were finally sold off to the Eagle Star Insurance Company in 1956, Ruperra had first been put up for sale in 1935, after the death of Courtenay Morgan left death duties of 30%. At that time it covered over 850 acres in total, including Home Farm at 450, and the buildings parklands, woods and plantations at approximately 400 acres. There were no offers. After the war, the castle having been accidentally burnt out in 1941, Ruperra was sold with the rest of the Tredegar Estates.

For the next five decades the Ruperra Estate would be gradually sold piecemeal. First the castle and parklands were sold to a Mrs Coles and then to a Mr Harrity, finally becoming a dairy farm in the ownership of Mr Des England in the 1970s. In 1998 the castle and outbuildings and 17 acres of grounds surrounding it, including the site of the historic gardens and the derelict glasshouse, were sold to a developer, Mr Barakat, whose housing

Ruperra 2004

application having been refused by Caerphilly Councillors, is at the time of this reprinting, 2008, appealing against the decision.

Having been managed as a commercial conifer plantation by the Eagle Star Insurance Company, the woods to the north of the castle, known as Coed Craig Ruperra, were sold in 1983 to another insurance company, Refuge Farms, which became United Friendly in the 1990s. In 2000, Ruperra Conservation Trust bought the woodland with public money and the intention of making it into a public amenity and returning it to its ancient woodland status as far as possible.

Today, if you stand on the ridge of Coed Craig Ruperra and look down at the four hundred year old castle and landscaped grounds, their beauty is still appealing. The former estate buildings, gardens, parklands and woodlands even in their state of increasing dilapidation are still an aesthetic tonic for anyone who is able to appreciate them and there are many, many people who do. Even the overgrown wildness of the once well tended land has a romantic charm of its own and the castle itself has become a dignified romantic ruin, full of the memories of the people who once gave it life. After the disastrous fire of 1941, Ruperra became increasingly a hidden and forgotten place. Its importance as a magnificent

Ruperra Castle from Coed Craig Ruperra Scrub clearance in the foreground.

example of historic heritage and beauty, emphasises the national disgrace that there are no urgent action plans to recover and preserve the elegance of the past and display to all the people the meaning of the place, its heritage, its architecture and its landscape.

Ruperra today. The south east tower collapsed in 1981. There are large cracks in the others.

The demise to this condition of exquisite ruin from a living working country estate in 1930 has been rapid and has been gathering pace as time goes on. You could say that as a result of the recent lack of care and instances of unsympathetic urbanisation in some parts of the surrounding countryside, the estate does not bear much resemblance to its former glory, even though Caerphilly County Borough Council has designated Ruperra as a Conservation Area and placed it in a Special Landscape Area

Even so, the 'spirit of place' is still there; a sensation that the family have only just left, perhaps for a few hours and that they will soon be back. The servants will be carrying out their duties and the woodsmen will be working at their tasks. And as we walk up to the top of Coed Ruperra, we are taken even further back into history treading where feet have trod for thousands of years, our eyes seeing the same sea and the same mountains. If only we could know exactly how these people felt. They were human beings; they must have felt the same way as we do.

After Ruperra Castle was built by Sir Thomas Morgan in 1626, famous and important people recognised the social standing of the Morgans and appreciated the beauty and grandeur of Ruperra. The house was 'fit for a king' when Charles I stayed with Sir Thomas's second son Sir Philip Morgan at Ruperra for four nights, looking for funds and support after his defeat in the Battle of Naseby in 1645. Hereford Castle was under siege by the Parliamentarian army and Charles' advisers were desperately trying to raise support to relieve it. Charles was also in secret negotiations with the Scots while at Ruperra and his advisers were scurrying to and fro.

In 1684 Thomas Dineley made a famous sketch of the castle when accompanying Henry Somerset, Lord Lieutenant of North and South Wales, Duke of Beaufort, President of the Council of Wales and the Marches and Lord Warden of the Marches, on his inspection of the County Militia. It is said that the reason for the tour this time was to rally support for Charles II following the growing confusion brought about by the religious and constitutional problems of his reign. Dineley described the view across the park from Cefn Mably thus.

"....to pass through a proud park of Deer below which leads hence to Ruperra, His Grace's lodgings and view the majesty of the old oaks."

Avenue of Oaks 2005

There are still oaks in the parkland, the ones seen here line the south west drive to the castle, some probably planted in the early 20th century, replacing earlier ones that had died. Now the whole estate is listed Grade II on the Register of Landscapes, Parks and Gardens of Special Historic Interest in Wales, published by Cadw / ICOMOS,

In 1804 Benjamin Heath Malkin MA FSA, writing more than a century later than Dineley in "the Scenery, Antiquities, and Biography of South Wales" described a view and an experience that we all know.

"From Ruperrah the gardener conducted me across the park. The prospect was uncommonly attractive. The harvest moon at the full was just risen. The effect of it shining on the Bristol Channel, with the bold hills of Somersetshire beyond, was in a high degree beautiful. The channel, though from 12 to 15 miles across, seemed but like an inland river. The mountain valley of Caerphilly, as you come upon the Newport Road, has a powerful effect upon the mind, as seen by a bright moonlight."

A view across the Bristol Channel. The oak tree in the centre of the picture fell in a storm in 2002.

CHAPTER TWO
WAS LIFE BETTER ONE HUNDRED YEARS AGO?

Although it was the gardener who had taken Benjamin Malkin across the park, it is not until nearly another century has passed that we have the first insight into what it was like actually to work on the estate. Fortunately for us William Beechey's diary provides just this insight. From 1899 to 1920 William wrote one or two lines every night at Ruperra Home Farm about what had happened that day. Some of the books have been destroyed, but those that are left give a delightful picture of a world gone by, where nothing much changed from year to year, particularly before the First World War and a feeling that nothing major ever would change.

An extract from the diary of October 30th 1901 'Little Stradling came here to work.' provides a link with those estate workers who were still alive at the end the 20th century. 'Little Stradling's younger brother Bert, aged 92 in 1984, loved Ruperra and gladly told his memories of working on the Estate. His and others' nostalgic talk of the days that are gone brings Ruperra alive for us. Local people today lovingly remember accounts by fathers, mothers and grandparents who were employed on the Ruperra Estate, who lived in an estate cottage, worked hard but at a leisurely pace, walked everywhere and thought nothing of it, grew their own vegetables and kept a pig and some chickens.

Today people coming in to the area to live, without any family memories are often amazed to find such a beautiful place, with its hidden ruin set in such a wonderful unspoilt countryside. The castle's cracked towers and empty windows are still warm with images of the days when it commanded a thriving country estate, with an army of servants busying to and fro making things run smoothly for Colonel Freddie Morgan, his family and visitors.

Most of the servants' memories conjure up an idyllic existence, like our own memories of childhood when the sun was always shining. Perhaps it is human nature to remember the pleasant things in life and to have a romantic view of when we were young. With hindsight, the disadvantages of life one hundred years ago are only too obvious, but almost all the people I spoke to, thought that their childhood was more pleasant and more healthy than that of children today.

By the beginning of the Second World War, however, the old order was already beginning to pass away and after the war a new way of life gathered speed until today it almost seems that we are not the same kind of people. Was life better one hundred years ago? And if so, better in what way? Working for the Morgan family of Tredegar at Ruperra would have had the same advantages and disadvantages as working for any large employer. The concentration of wealth in the hands of one family is not so different from that of present day corporations. Perhaps the reader will have to make up his or her own mind as to whether working 'under' Ruperra was a good or a bad thing.

Recent research has found that in this country at the present time, unlike even fifty years ago, there is now the same disparity between rich and poor as there was a hundred years ago. The extremely rich today however, have little knowledge or perception of how the other half lives, unlike the wealthy families of the great agricultural estates of 1900, who lived with their employees' families all around them, and felt some responsibility for their welfare, in the absence of state help.

There were still people who thought things were not right however. Two local stories, which may or may not be the whole truth but were obviously believed by some at the time, were said to illustrate the ruthless way in which the Morgan family continued to build up their already vast property and wealth.

'At one time, Ty Cornel (see the map on pages 5 and 6) belonged to a Mr Davies, a stonemason working for the Tredegar estates who had built the house himself. Now whether he'd had an accident or whether he was just ill we don't know, but he was off work for some time. The agent called, the wife came to the door and they passed the time of day. Then the agent said 'How's Mr Davies?' 'Oh he's still abed, Sir.' 'Oh I'm sorry' And then he put his foot over the threshold and said 'If he's not back in work by Monday morning this house belongs to Lord Tredegar.' And that was how the house became part of the Tredegar Estate.' *However, the house is shown on the Tithe map of 1841 on land belonging to the Tredegar Estate anyway.*

Another story concerns the land in Draethen where the Cardiff Rural District Council houses now stand. It was common land divided up into gardens for the Houses opposite,called 'The Row.' 'To protect the workers' gardens, Lord

Tredegar put a wall around it but then he later sold the land as his own.'
Again he would have been the overall landowner of the common land anyway, but these stories indicate how some people felt.

It would seem that until the death of Courtenay in 1935, individual members of the Tredegar family had been mindful of their duties to their tenants and servants for whom they provided employment and there are many accounts of their generosity. In fact there is evidence that they were too generous for their own good when, in the late 20s and 30s a time of poverty for many, they decided not to increase the rents despite their own financial problems.

With roots in an ancient Welsh family and the accompanying traditions of generosity and hospitality, the Morgans throughout history probably took their elated position seriously, although without more research no early examples can be given. Godfrey, Lord Tredegar from 1875 to 1913, firmly believed that with great wealth and power came great responsibilities and there are very many instances of his public and personal generosity and of his sympathetic and sensitive nature. In a collection entitled the "Wit and Wisdom of Lord Tredegar" published by the Western Mail in 1912 Godfrey had this to say for example about his time in the Crimea.

Godfrey Lord Tredegar

'Before going out to the Crimea, I was accustomed to see,......farmers looking happy and contented..........but since the war commenced, I have seen the other side of the picture. I have seen an army march into an hostile country,   and there, in a few hours, all was desolation, one stone not being left on another, and the people made slaves to the invaders. How thankful we ought to be that we are not suffering at the hands of an invading army.' *(From a speech given at the Newport Agricultural Show, 1855.*

He rewarded his lifelong friend, Richard Stratton, with the very prestigious Dyffryn Farm in Newport. Stratton had saved his life when wounded in the Crimean War, by putting him under a gun carriage for protection. William Huthwaite, from Whitby in Yorkshire (1824 – 1891) and Godfrey's butler at Ruperra Castle, had been taken to the Crimea with him. Godfrey and

William were both in their early twenties at the time. William and his family lived first at Minorca Cottages and then at East Lodge, where he died a widower in 1891, having been well rewarded. His descendants, the James family, still live in the area and treat their connection with Ruperra with much affection.

Jeannie Wilson, (née Greenway) can remember being taken as a child to see the statue of Godfrey in the Hayes in Cardiff and gazing up at it with awe. A tenant famously remarked 'If I would worship anyone but God it would be Lord Tredegar.'

William Huthwaite in his army uniform

Many Ruperra employees remembered acts of caring before there was legislation to enforce them. Bert Stradling, from Rudry, after starting as an odd job boy on the Estate in 1906, was apprenticed to the building industry by the Tredegar Estate. Mary Thomas, a servant at Ruperra in the 1920s mentioned how Courtenay, Lord Tredegar, would always acknowledge you in the grounds and that 'when Colonel Freddie was in residence and the Machen farm tenants came over (probably to pay their rent,) he would give them soup and dripping. If somebody had an accident in the parish, the Morgans would have soup sent round, and they'd send their own beer from the cellars at the castle.' Another servant remembered that once a year, the workers' wives and mothers would go to the Hollybush and be given a bolt of cloth. On the other hand, the domestic staff at the castle had to buy their own uniforms.

Colonel Freddie

Ethel Ackland (née Mayho) who lived at Ruperra Park Lodge for many years until the 1990s, remembered that Lord Tredegar used to give Christmas gifts to his employees according to their rank, ranging from a leg of pork to a goose to a rabbit! John Phillips who used to farm Clearwell Farm in Michaelstone y Fedw said 'Mr Rae at the Hollybush was in charge of all the materials that the farmers needed to secure their property. You had to provide the labour yourself, but Mr

Rae would provide the stakes and fencing and so on. If you offered him any money for them he would say that he never accepted tips, but that his wife did!' *The Tredegar Estate employed a man known as Johnny Gatehanger who as his name suggested would go round hanging the gates the farmers would have collected from Mr Rae.*

Kath Ayres from the Draethen remembered that 'you could get all your repairs done for nothing. You'd only have to ring up the Tredegar Office and you'd have all your paint and paper. There was a lot of good. There was an article in the South Wales Argus about my grandfather *(Edwin Jones)* and Mr McKinnon and Mr Price Iron Bridge. When they came to the end of their working lives, they were up in their 70's. My grandfather had worked for Ruperra all his life. The pension from the Tredegar Estate was 10 shillings a week and the old age pension was 10 shillings, which he'd collect from Mrs Webb who kept the Post Office down in Lower Machen. He died in 1953 and he had the Tredegar pension up until he died.

Mary Thomas recalled how the old employees used to like to talk about the old days. 'When the Spooners went to live to the Draethen, the old gent,

LONG SERVICE QUARTETTE

FOUR members of Ruperra Castle estate staff have a record of service totalling nearly two hundred years. They are

Mr. Angus McKinnon, formerly head gardener, now custodian of the picturesque castle, 52 years;

Mr Alfred Beacon, head gamekeeper 55 years;

Mr Edwin Jones, blacksmith, 54 years; and

Mr. William Price, gamekeeper, 34 years.

The first-named, a typical Scot, took pride in the gardens and grounds, which are flanked on three sides by woods. He was a familiar figure at Tredegar House Servants' Ball, and his jocular manner makes him a friend of everybody. Now he receives a well-earned pension.

Like the other three servants, he has served under three heads of the Tredegar family. Hundreds who have walked or driven along the Michaelstone-road skirting the Castle Park must have been impressed by the large number of firs, which give the place an air of seclusion and peace. They have an interesting history.

Years ago the first Viscount Tredegar, of Balaclava fame, saw a number of fir trees at Cheltenham, and he was so attracted by them that he decided to make them a feature of Ruperra Park. Mr. McKinnon, his head gardener, supervised the planting of the saplings.

In the bad old days, Mr. Beacon, the head gamekeeper, had many an encounter with armed poachers. He still bears the scars of shot wounds. Ruperra is in Glamorgan, and at that time cases from the estate were heard in a public-house at Caerphilly That was, of course, long before the police court was built there.

(*Joseph*) he was crippled with arthritis, used to struggle if it was a nice day, down to that bench by the whitewashed cottage, the other side of the road from the Old Brewhouse. And I used to hope and pray when I'd come home on the bus from Caerphilly that he wouldn't be sitting there because Lord knows what time I'd get home then! My sister would come to see where I was! And Mr Jones, Kath Ayres' grandfather would catch you too and they would both tell you stories all about Ruperra. It was their little world. They used to get up to such tricks there'.

A young family living in the Preserve were the Greenways. William Greenway's daughter Jeannie said 'My father was a policemen and my mother, Anita Everson, a maid to the Bowen-Rees family at Holly House. They wanted to marry, so, because there was a cottage to go with the job of game keeper at Ruperra, my dad became a keeper in 1905 and stayed until 1912. My eldest sister was born there in 1907 and Colonel Freddie Morgan called to see the new baby and asked if he might choose her name. He was obviously keen on opera because he chose the name Brunhilde, which did not go down very well with my parents. They compromised on Bryn-Hilda which was shortened to Brynie. The Colonel gave the new baby a beautiful fine lawn and lace christening gown and bonnet, which has been used for all the family since that time and has travelled across the Atlantic many times.'

Brynie aged 98 with her Canadian great grandson wearing the gown.

The Preserve from across the Park

The Morgans were very mindful of saving their servants' souls. The morning service at St Michael and All Angels' Church in Lower Machen had been moved to 11 15 a.m by 1875 because the servants, so it was said, couldn't clear away breakfast and get to church by 11 o'clock! The Reverend Augustus Morgan,

Lower Machen Church

brother of Charles, the First Baron Tredegar had received the living of Lower Machen Church in 1828 and lived at Machen House. A year later, the carriage drive from the Castle to Lower Machen over the Iron Bridge, was built.

Godfrey Lord Tredegar, although a staunch Anglican himself was not averse to helping members of other religious denominations and spoke out for tolerance of all religions even non Christian. In 1893 he helped the members of a Risca chapel, which had become too small for the congregation with the industrial immigration in the late 19th century. They decided to ask Lord Tredegar to let them have a small piece of land already donated by him to Risca as playing fields. The first time they went to Ruperra, he was not at home. The next time they did not let a surprise fall of snow deter them from journeying again over Ochrwyth to Ruperra. They were invited into the Castle by a footman and asked to wait in the hall way. Eventually they overcame Lord Tredegar's reluctance to give them the land and before they left, a manservant brought three bowls of soup to warm them up for the long walk home. Moriah Chapel, a huge building on the main road in Risca, still stands and its members still work very hard today helping the community.

In 1861 Godfrey donated the building stones for Tirzah chapel in Michaelstone-y-Fedw. The total cost was £500 with seating for 350. The Tredegar agent, William Treharne Rees of Holly House Farm, and a highly respected Baptist, paid for the schoolroom there. A tablet to this effect was placed on the Holly House family pew in the chapel.

Immigrant workers swelled these congregations but in any case local people had large families. Bert Stradling was one of eleven, but five of them died young, mostly of colds he said, which turned to pneumonia. He didn't remember much of the deaths as he was one of the youngest, but he thought that people didn't dwell much on the loss of their children. The attitude was 'As long as he's got a good full belly and a good pair of boots he'll survive.' But perhaps that was just bravado. Mothers and fathers must have grieved deeply for the little ones who were gone, even if they were soon replaced.

FUNERAL AT MACHEN.

Late Miss Janie McKinnon.

The funeral of the late Miss Janie McKinnon, youngest daughter of Mr. and Mrs. Angus McKinnon (head gardener Ruperra Castle Gardens) took place on Monday at the Parish Church, Lower Machen. The Rev. S. M. Davies (rector of the parish) officiated at the church and the graveside, assisted by the Rev. G. R. Picton (curate).

In the church the hymns, "Christ will gather in His own," "Thy way, not mine, O Lord," were sung, a full choir being present. As the cortege left the church Mrs. Newton Wade played the Dead March in "Saul."

The coffin, which was of panelled oak, bore the inscription, "Margaret J. McKinnon, died June 17, 1915, aged 21 years." The bearers were Messrs. T. Young, W. Gratton, D. C. Price, P. R. Lewis, L. John, and T. T. Price.

The chief mourners were: Mr. Angus McKinnon (father), Lance-Corporal C. McKinnon, Private Bert McKinnon, Mr. Douglas McKinnon (brothers), Mr. Harry Basham (brother-in-law). Others present were: Messrs. Newton Wade, F. Stratton, W. R. Lloyd, J. Basham, W. Broom, J. Duff, J. Rosser, G. Beeston, G. D. Inkin, A. Rymer, T. Morgan, W. T. Webb, J. Ashton, G. Lewis, T. Watkins, J. Jones, Private W. Beeston, W. Beeston (sen.), B. Jones, and others.

Floral tributes were sent from the following: Father and mother; sister and brothers; Nettie and Harry; Mr. J. Basham and family; the Hon. Mr. and Mrs. F. Morgan (Boughrood Castle); Mr. and Mrs. L. Forestier-Walker and family; Mr. and Mrs. Newton Wade; Mr. and Mrs. E. Perrott and family; Mr. and Mrs. Davidson and Jack; Rev. and Mrs. S. M. Davies; Mrs. Jones and family; Nellie Rymer; All at Lower Machen Post Office; Gladys Gratton and May Richards; Mr. and Mrs. A. E. Jones; E. Bosson, Tredegar Park; Ruperra Gardens; Mr. and Mrs. W. H. John and family; Mr. and Mrs. G. Beeston and family; Mr. and Mrs. J. Duff and family; Machen Branch of the Girls' Friendly Society; Machen Cricket Club; Machen Flower Show Committee.

The arrangements were carried out by Mr. T. Davies, Machen.

June 22nd, 1915.

Tuberculosis hit rich and poor alike. In spite of all his wealth, Evan, Lord Tredegar from 1935 to 1949 contracted it, and in spite of all the healthy food and fresh air at Ruperra, two of head gardener Angus McKinnon's daughters died of it: Janie in June 1915 aged 21 and Mary in August 1915 aged 26..

Godfrey Lord Tredegar was one of eleven children who all survived to adulthood, but in 1792, the Morgan family had come close to running out of male heirs. Jane Morgan's husband Sir Charles Gould, granted the name and arms of Morgan by royal licence, transformed the Estate into an industrial and commercial enterprise. In 1859, their grandson, Sir Charles Morgan Robinson Morgan became the First Baron Tredegar. Both his sons, Godfrey and Frederick seem to have been mindful of their employees' welfare.

Freddie's son Courtenay may have provided work by refurbishing Ruperra but his luxurious life style in the face of crippling death duties, and the national economic situation prevented him and his son Evan safeguarding their inheritance.

Back in 1900 however you could not be blamed for thinking that the old order would continue forever.

CHAPTER THREE ESTATE HOUSES AND THEIR OCCUPANTS

The traveller can still see a great many surviving features of the old Ruperra Estate, including houses. Some of these are in ruins, some are still standing but with familiar Tredegar design features and others are enlarged and altered out of all recognition. Like many houses on other estates, Tredegar houses had authentic dormer windows and stone decoration around the top of their other windows. The front doors of the smaller ones often had a little open porch with a two sided tiled roof. For the most part, by the beginning of the 20th century, the roofs were of stone rather than thatch since the Morgans owned most of the stone quarries in the district. Most of the following houses appear on the Tithe maps of Rudry and Michaelstone-y-Fedw of 1839 and 1841, but the exact date of construction of some of the smaller ones are unknown.

Machen House

The large houses near Ruperra which were on Tredegar land but not part of the Ruperra Estate were often occupied by members of the Morgan family or the more important agents of the Tredegar Estate. Today some of them are listed buildings being historically and architecturally significant in their own right.

Machen House for example, is Georgian, Plas Machen and Machen Fach, Tudor. Sir Foster Stedman, one of the agricultural agents for the Tredegar Estate lived at Machen House, later retiring to the Garth, now the Friendly Fox Public House in Rhiwderin, where John Storrar, the Tredegar agent for the urban properties had lived previously. Some of the Stratton family lived and farmed at Plas Machen until 1926, hence the name 'Stratton Hill' still in use for that part of the A468 by Plas Machen just before the railway bridge.

The Ruperra farm bailiffs, head game keepers, head grooms and head gardeners either lived in buildings in the castle grounds or in fairly large estate houses. These were Ruperra Home Farm and Gwernleyshon Farm where the farm bailiffs lived, the Preserve, where the head gamekeeper lived, the

Parkfield House

Hollybush Inn where after 1918 a head forester lived and Ironbridge Cottage where another gamekeeper and at one time a policeman lived. Before moving to the Bothy in the castle grounds in 1910, Mr McKinnon, the head gardener lived in Park Field House opposite the church in Lower Machen. Once a school, it was attended by Dr William Price, Rudry's most famous son, born in 1800, who introduced cremation to the modern developed world.

Trusted employees lived at West Lodge, East Lodge and Ruperra Park Lodge where it is said, they, or their wives were responsible for unlocking the gates into the estate when the Morgan family wished to enter or leave. When she was a girl, Winifred Knibbs,(née Ackland) lived at Ruperra Park Lodge which is at the entrance to the Ruperra Drive to the Castle. She was fascinated by the stories her mother, Ethel told her about life on the Estate in the 19th century.

Ruperra Park Lodge
Ethel and Winifred

'The Lodge was built in the 1860s. They say it took two years to build. Before Lord Tredegar built the new drive *(now the public footpath that we walk along today)*, he would use the old back lane *(now the public bridleway)* to approach the castle. When he went past the houses along the lane the people living there were meant to go inside because he would most likely have important visitors who mustn't see his tenants. The story goes that there was once an orchard along here stretching from the ruined cottage to where the steps are in the wall where the black door used to be. *(Now a five bar gate)*. One day Lord Tredegar was passing there with some important person and the woman of the house who was hard of hearing and wasn't aware of the approaching carriage, was still outside gathering apples from the orchard. The story goes that the family were thrown out of the cottage and the orchard chopped down. There were still a few apple trees at our Parkwall Cottage when we went there and a few plum trees but the orchard itself was gone.

When the new road was built the cottages were now down behind a wall bordering the new road. There were steps over the wall to access the estate. The Ruperra Park Lodge gates at the highway end of the drive were kept locked all the time except to let Lord Tredegar and his family through. Whoever lived there was a key holder and had to be there at his beck and call. This would be a more important person than the ones who lived in the cottages. Either a groomsman or gamekeeper would live there and their wives opened the gates.

The West Lodge people were key holders as well. West Lodge was home to a succession of employees who held strategic positions on the estate. The new road was cobbled, and you can see the remains of this starting at West Lodge and going along the drive behind the Castle today. Considering everything, including the soldiers' vehicles during the war, the drive has lasted well.

West Lodge

My mother Ethel was never frightened living there on her own even until the 1990s. When she was younger she used to go out in the night to the Park to collect wood for the fire. My father used to play hell with her but she always said that in the dark you will see if anybody's coming towards you - you'll see the shadow on the ground. People used to have hobnailed boots too so that you'd know who was walking by the sound of their boots. It was quiet because there was no traffic about and the roads were rough and everybody walked differently, slow, fast, heavy and so on and could be recognised. And of course everybody knew everybody else.'

At Home Farm lived the Beecheys of whom we shall hear more. Elwyn Edwards' mother was a Beechey, the sister of William who kept the diary. She was born at Home Farm and in the 30s used to take Elwyn to visit her other brother Tom Beechey, at East Lodge. East Lodge was an interesting house with lots of dummy windows, it seems. Unfortunately a tree fell on it in a storm in 1913 and although it was repaired, (in the 1940s Thelma Clifford from Michaelstone lived there) later it was demolished and replaced by the modern Ruperra House.

Elwyn says, 'I remember the long walk, as a small boy of six, across the fields from Lower Machen. We would always stop to talk to the Prices at Iron Bridge. Mr Price was a gamekeeper who had an iron hook for a hand which used to frighten my sister and me. After passing the house we would walk through a tunnel of trees where there were always rabbits running about. We turned left on the main road and went through a little gate further along where we passed through another tunnel of conifers leading us out eventually to East Lodge.'

East Lodge with the fallen tree.

Elwyn remembers tales his mother told at this time, one which has always stayed in his mind as some stories do. It was about a man, who might have lived when Elwyn's mother herself was little. It seems he was very cruel to animals and to his own children. One day he had his come uppance when some overgrown brambles hit him in the face and caused his eye to fall out on the path in front of him! A moral tale possibly!

Iron Bridge Cottage was built soon after the construction of the Iron Bridge over the Rhymney River in 1829. Although not included on the Tithe Map of 1839, the house was recorded on the Census of 1841. The Iron bridge now listed Grade II is a fine example of an early cast iron bridge. Over the years the Glamorgan Constabulary as well as gamekeepers lived at the cottage. Sergeant John Ashton and PC Carpenter before Mr Price the gamekeeper.

Iron bridge Cottage

'The head keeper' said Bert Stradling who started work on the estate in 1906 'always lived in the Preserve and was in charge of rearing the birds. Alf Beeton was keeper at one time when I was there, after him was Reckless, then Greenway, then Thomas and then Blackburn.

Winifred Ackland remembers the Blackburns with affection. 'Mrs Blackburn was often coming up to the Ruperra drive from the Preserve wearing her dark brown fox fur around her neck. Of course when you're only so big you'd look at these things carefully and the fox fur used to fascinate me. It had a very good head on it hanging down and it used to shine and the eyes were good. She always wore long skirts too. She used to go to post letters at Ty Cornel. All the neighbours along the drive and in the Park were very sociable, visiting and chatting to each other daily. It was a happy time.'

Often employees would move from one property to another as their jobs on the estate warranted. Tom Pembridge who served in many roles at the Castle, also lived at West Lodge, then in the stable block at Ruperra and then at Beech Cottage in Draethen. Sergeant Penny and his family lived in Iron Bridge Cottage and Ruperra Park Lodge at various times. The Huthwaites and the Beecheys moved around too. Morris Jenkins, a gardener on the estate, had lived at Graig View on the Draethen-Michaelstone road before moving to West Lodge where his daughter Edna, (now Dix) was born

Some of the many smaller cottages around the estate can still be seen, with a charm of their own. Some are altered out of all recognition, some others are now sadly in ruins and some have disappeared altogether. Along the road to Draethen from the Maenllwyd Inn the two Cwm Leyshon cottages can still be seen, one of them now called the Retreat and neither of them

Cwm Leyshon Cottage

little cottages any more. Next to them is Yew Tree cottage with its distinctive flat roof, a relatively modern addition.

In Draethen itself, Spring Chase, the Trout Farm, was built on the site of a gamekeeper's house, and further along from Glan y Nant and Beech cottage is The Row, a terrace of small cottages, now Listed Buildings. Kath Ayres lived in the house at the end of The Row where her parents and her grandparents had lived. 'When the estate was sold we thought a lot about not buying the house, then about buying it and Dad said well its only the three of us; (it became four of us when I got married mind at 39!) we've got 2 bedrooms what more do we want? Not one of us wanted to go from here you see.' When the estate was sold in 1956 her father bought the house for £26. Apart from her time away in the WAAF during World War Two, Kath lived there all her life until she died in 1998.

Taken from the Hollybush Inn. The Toll house has now gone.

Kath Ayres house first left

Doris Oram who lives in Number 3 The Row, remembered both Mrs Brittan and Mrs Lloyd doing teas in their houses in The Row in Draethen. Doris said 'Mrs Lloyd had been housekeeper at the Bothy and people said that her son Billy was the exact likeness of Lord Tredegar. Mrs Lloyd and Billy lived next door but one to Kath Ayres in The Row free of charge. She was a dear little old lady and there was no harm in Billy, although he wasn't quite all there. After she died Billy Lloyd took in a man and his wife who got him out from his own house and made him live in a shed in the field at the back of the garden. I knew Billy Lloyd from when I was a little girl so when I cooked tea every night I used to do enough for him as well and send my son round to the shed with it in a little dish. I didn't like to think that he was up there and not having a meal everyday. Somebody did him a good turn though, because they reported it and he was taken to an old people's home in Caerphilly where he was treated really well and brought to visit his friends in Draethen dressed really nicely. But those other people never had any luck after that. They both died young.'

Marion Beeston and Doris Oram at No3 The Row.

While Lower Machen itself was not within the boundary of the Ruperra Esate, almost all of the old houses in Lower Machen were Tredegar Estate houses. The row of cottages, originally thatched, with the Forge at one end

and Volland House at the other, were improved at the same time as Courtenay Morgan's refurbishment at Ruperra in the early 20th century.

Margery Jones whose hundredth birthday occurred in April 2005 was born at the Forge. Volland House, on the right of each picture on the previous page, is where the Beeston family have lived for over a hundred years. Marian Beeston's father, Bert is the little boy standing on the right of the group. Most of the Beeston men worked on the Tredegar Estate and some of them at Ruperra as well. Marion Beeston says that her father 'worked as a carpenter for the Tredegar Estate until it was sold in the 50s. His father and his brother Will had been stone masons on the estate.'

The Post Office in Lower Machen was run by the Webbs, and by Mrs Webb on her own, after William died. Later Marion Beeston's mother was the Post Mistress, seen here flanked by Jinny and Lizzie, (cousins of Elwyn Edwards) who used to deliver the post. The Head Postmaster had come up from Newport for a presentation. Mrs Beeston died at the age of 103 in 1999

Returning along the road to the Hollybush Inn in Draethen and from there to the Michaelston-y-Fedw road, can be seen Alltfarian and Spout Cottage, Graig View Cottage, Tresguthan, Gwern y Goetre and Minorca Cottages, all of which were occupied by estate workers. Some of the Beechey family lived at Minorca Cottages, as did William Huthwaite, one

Spout Cottage with Alltfarian behind.

Spring Cottage

time butler to Godfrey, Lord Tredegar.

Further into Michaelstone there were many more estate cottages and Jim Spring lived in one by the old bridge. There were seven Bridge Cottages in the 1901 Census with another cottage called Bridge Shop. Next to one of them, now called Spring Cottage, is a field accessed by a stile where a rushing little stream runs through the remaining stone work of the bapistry belonging to Tirzah Chapel, now demolished, up the road. The stream then runs under the road and joins a bigger stream under Michaelstone Bridge, in turn joining the Rhymney River. Standing there on a quiet afternoon it is easy to be transported back into the world of Alfred Wheeley, Jim Spring, George Lewis, John Rees and Alfred Morgan who all lived around there and worked on the estate. Alfred Morgan was a foreman carpenter. The Bridge shop was kept by Edward Bishop, a market gardener.

On the road from Lisvane, on the western approach to the Ruperra Estate is Llwyn Celyn which has recently been considerably enlarged. Another estate family, the Edwards, lived there after moving from Ruperra Park Lodge. Mr Edwards had been one of the top four groomsmen at the Castle and was presented with a silver mounted hoof from one of Lord Tredegar's favourite horses buried in the field beyond the deer sheds. Mrs Edwards, who was the daughter of Mr Reckless the gamekeeper, eventually gave this hoof to Wnifred Knibb's mother Ethel at Ruperra Park Lodge. Winifred remembers that 'Mrs Edwards lived into her 90's. She was very well read and had books on everything and all jars around the room with snakes preserved in them. She used to walk to Caerphilly in her 70s to buy fish heads for her cats. Her daughter, Olive went to a private school.'

Llwyn Celyn

Nearer to the estate on the Lisvane road can still be seen Ffald Gerrig and Ty Cornel. At Ffald Gerrig, the Stradlings lived in the left hand side of the cottage, while another family lived on the right hand side. Bert Stradling who lived there for nearly ninety years, described 'the separate stairs to go up from each side, which then met at the top! Then in the 1920s we had the whole house to ourselves.' When the estate was sold to Eagle Star in 1956 Bert and his mother

Ffald Gerrig

were able to buy Ffald Gerrig but were obliged by the Council to put in a back door – the beginning of Health and Safety regulations – but, said Bert, no-one from the Council came to check it! The little building, still there at the end of the house, was a blacksmith's shop and the horses would pull up on the other side of the road where there was also a small pigsty. Bert and his wife Minnie kept a sweet shop at one time and often in summer they would sit at the gate selling blackcurrants from their prolific blackcurrant bushes.

Ty Cornel

Ty Cornel, as its name implies stands on the corner of the road from Lisvane to Rudry where it descends to the Cwm. It had a corner rounded off at some time in the 19th century. Teams of horses pulling heavy loads were not able to negotiate the sharp bend and so a practical solution was sought. Who authorized the change and whether the occupants had a say in the matter is not known as yet

Along the Ruperra drive from Ty Cornel were four cottages called Parkwall, of which we shall hear more later and in one of which Tom Morgan's family lived. Bert Stradling takes up the story. 'Tom Morgan's family were masons and it was their job to look after the dry wall right round the Estate. Tom's wife had been a lady's maid at Ruperra.' According to Mary and Enid Thomas, the son, also

Tom, 'was not at all like his father who was a small wiry little fellow.' *Readers may draw their own conclusions from this. Bert continues.* 'Tom was a big fellow and grew up to be a marvellous platform speaker. He used to do a lot of speaking for the Tredegar family at elections. Colonel Freddie Morgan was MP for Monmouthshire until 1906. Tom (*junior*) when he reached adulthood went to live at Ty Cornel and renamed it Woodbine Cottage. *(It's now called Ty Cornel again.)* It was a lovely little cottage with a little boiler place on the outside and a toilet by the greenhouse. Tom had a letterbox put in the wall because he was secretary of the Oddfellows club in the Hollybush Inn and had a lot of post. When he moved from there up to the Griffin he had a letterbox put in the Church wall there too!'

Tom Morgan's granddaughter, Elaine, remembers her father telling her that 'when my grandmother (Tom's wife) had appendicitis, Lord Tredegar called in a London specialist who operated on her in Ty Cornel. There was no electricity there of course so the whole operation was performed with only oil lamps and candles for light'. *Bert Stradling's mother from across the road at Ffald Gerrig was in there holding a candle.*

Bert remembered that 'Tom Morgan held a 'smoking concert' at the Griffin in Rudry (*which had been bought by now from the Plymouth Estate by the Tredegar Estate*) to collect money for the people injured in the collieries. And he was a big man with the Bristol and West Insurance Society. Men paid in money every month to the club. This was called 'paying the club'.

Tom went very sudden with pneumonia. The daughter was very ill and they were expecting her to go any minute and they didn't think of poor old Tom. He was too fat though. Anyway he went, not the daughter.' *Tom's granddaughter adds,* 'My aunt had meningitis (my father said she was never the same again) so they probably were more worried about her.' *Tom*

Morgan's son Gwyn kept the Griffin Inn for the rest of his life and his granddaughter kept it until the 1990s when it was developed for housing. The Griffin Inn was probably the oldest pub in the area. There is a local story that being near St James' Church in Rudry, it catered for medieval pilgrims journeying to St James of Compostella in Spain.

Only one of the four Parkwall cottages along the Ruperra Drive had its own name, Ty Gibbon. By now two of them have disappeared completely, and the position of one of these is now shown only by a yew tree at the side of the track which in itself is difficult to identify.

The remaining two cottages are now in ruins, falling into disrepair when the

The last remaining Parkwall Cottage in 1950 and in 2005

estate was sold in the 50s and planning permission for restoration being unobtainable in later years. Only one ruin can be seen from the track. Here are 'before and after' pictures of it; the one on the left shows how it looked just after the estate was sold in the 50s when the Orams lived there. Pearl Llewellyn (née Oram) says that her father had to mend the roof himself with thatch, since supplies from the Tredegar Estate were no longer obtainable and he couldn't afford tiles. Before the Orams, the Miles family had lived there. The picture on the right shows the ruins of this cottage as seen today along the Ruperra Drive.
As for the other ruined cottage, Ty Gibbon, Roy Hawkins moved into it when he was three, in 1927. 'I can always remember my grandfather Hawkins holding me

Ty Gibbon

in his arms while we looked at the chicken run around the back of the cottage. My mother was a very strong woman. Once because there was no one around to help her, she carried some full sacks of corn into the barn! I can remember that when Lord Tredegar *(Courtenay)* was staying at the Castle, the Union Jack would be flying there. He'd be there for maybe a week but I didn't go much towards the Castle as a child; I'd go more towards Ffald Gerrig where my relations, the Stradlings, lived.'

He only moved away from there in the 50s when his mother and father were getting on, his younger brother had left home and his older brother had died. Although the family home is now a ruin, Roy still has a small holding there, set well back from the track. Until this track was laid in the 1860s Ty Gbbon and the Parkwall cottage next to it were on either side of the old track. The cottage was six feet below the level of the old drive. This drive is now Public Bridleway number 14, starting from the highway by Ruperra Park Lodge and going to Draethen through the woods.

When Mary and Enid Thomas lived in Park wall, (in the cottage with only the yew tree left) 't here was a spring in the woods. You could see it bubbling up. It was lovely water. Icy cold. One man living up in the woods the other side of the road from Cwm Leyshon used to go there every evening and carry his clean water from there.'

After Mary and Enid's family had moved to Cwm Leyshon, their 'Aunty Matty' and her husband remained at Parkwall.. Mary said 'When they got old, Lord Tredegar built a lovely addition to that house so that they could sleep down stairs. Mr McKinnon the head gardener used to come over from the Bothy in the Castle grounds to bring them morning sticks for the fire and vegetables. Auntie would give him some hot beer.'

Glan y Nant Farm, further down the road from Ty Cornel to Cefn Mably had been part of the Cefn Mably Estate until bought by the Morgans in 1920. David Jones who lived there until he died in January 2005, said that his relations from Began could remember a carriage and pair regularly going up the road to the south entrance of the castle. He also remembered a forester, called Williams who in the 30s, looked after the avenue of oak trees on the south west drive.

The Avenue of Oaks 2005

It was a settled, comfortable way of life, having a house and a job on the Ruperra Estate. It was important to like what you were doing or it might have seemed tedious, but as far as we are told most of the estate workers enjoyed their work very much and were very involved in the life and well being of the estate. They felt secure, living and working 'under Ruperra.' The next chapter gives us a detailed account of what that work involved.

CHAPTER FOUR
AN INTRODUCTION TO THE TWENTIETH CENTURY

The discovery of William Beechey's diary was one of those events which make the study of local history so rewarding. Here was an example of the work of those valuable people who must write down something about what happened in the day. William's diary records twenty years of information about the lives of the people of the Ruperra Estate and the events which affected them. His interests covered the Morgan family themselves at the Castle – Colonel Freddie Morgan, MP for Monmouthshire was in residence when the entries start in 1899, - national and international affairs, his own social life, his family's health as well as the work at Ruperra Home Farm where he lived, together with anything else that caught his fancy.

The Beecheys 1895. Children from L to R Rowland, Harry, Gwladys, Rosa

For the purposes of this book, I have made a very brief selection of the entries. The original diaries consisting of 270 pages were lent to me for copying by the late Mr Herbie Spring of Draethen, into whose treasured possession they came.

The Diary

In the Census returns of 1891 William Beechey is described as an agricultural labourer from Castletown, Monmouthshire, speaking both English and Welsh and living at Llanvedw which was probably a farm cottage attached to Home Farm proper. By the 1901 Census he had moved to the Home Farm and was

Ruperra Home Farm

described in the returns for that year as 'shepherd on farm' although as we shall see, he did much more than look after sheep. His family believes that he was a bailiff and perhaps he became a bailiff later, but of course the census returns for the years after 1901 are not yet available so this cannot be verified at present. In both censuses there were several other members of the Beechey family mentioned as living close by.

William must have been quite tired after his work each day especially as he got older, but he still sat down every evening to write a few sentences.

1899

March 13th Put 6 hens to sit in box. Rosa got shingles. Doctor been to see mother. Ivor bad in bed. *(Ivor Coslett adopted by and brought up by the Beecheys. He made a great impression on everyone by his capacity for hard work.)* Finished digging the garden. Mr and Mrs F Morgan *(Colonel Freddie's son Frederick and his wife Dorothy)* came to the Castle. They are not coming to Machen House. *(Machen House had been enlarged in 1831 for the Reverend Augustus Morgan, rector of Lower Machen Church, and son of Sir Charles Morgan)* Jim Spring sowing oats the left side of New Georgy. *(A field at Home Farm – see the map pages 5 and 6)*

Ivor Coslett

March 14th Shoot in the Deer park. Sacking all the men at Cefn Mabley. All but five. *(Unfortunately there are no reasons given for this. Cefn Mably was the home of the Kemys-Tynte family from the late 16th until the early 20th century. It was joined in ownership at one time in the late 17th century with Ruperra and eventually bought by the Tredegar Estate in 1920. Used as a hospital in the 20th century, it*

was burnt out in 1995, then restored and converted into flats in 2000 with forty new houses built in the grounds where many mature broadleaf trees were felled.)
Mr Reaves here today and preaching at the Draethen tonight. The turkeys began to lay

Sheep in the snow in the Clump Field in 1898, taken by Miss Millar

March 23rd Cleaned out the bin house. The rats are there bad. A lamb died in the Clump Field. *(See the map on pages 6 & 7).*

March 23rd The new Keeper looking all round the place with Mr Rymer. *(A farm bailiff who lived at Gwern Leyshon Farm)*

April 3$^{rd.}$ Cardiff Races Colonel Morgan's horse won. Torpedo. Turned out a fine day for Easter Monday. Mr Thomas not well not going to Tirzah to preach in Anniversary services. *(Tirzah. A very flourishing Baptist chapel in Michaelstone y Fedw where William Beechey was made a deacon in 1903. Kath Ayres from the Draethen said 'On Whit Tuesday there used to be the tea and a concert at Tirzah chapel in Michaelstone. Everyone from the chapel would go up to the Castle on the Tuesday morning and they'd cut down the whole of that bank to the north of Ruperra Drive with all coloured rhododendrons and they'd get a horse and cart to bring them down to Tirzah.' Chapel members included the Beecheys, the Springs, the Spooners, the Huthwaites and the Esthers. Demolished in the 1960s, only the graveyard and the baptistry now remain. Baptism was by total immersion and the brook by the baptistry was damned to provide the necessary depth of water. See Chapter 3)*

April 4th Mrs Morgan been dead 8 years. Died 1891 at Ruperra Castle 53 years of age. *(Colonel Freddie's wife Charlotte)* Killed the last pig. Sold 7 black sheep

April 6th The new keeper came today. The new keepers goods came all the way from Stroud in a one horse van. The horse brought it all the way its own self. *(The strength of this horse obviously impressed William.)* Mr and Mrs Mundy came to the castle today. *(Colonel Freddie's daughter Violet married to Basil Mundy)*

April 8th Cut up tonight a old piece of cart made over 80 years ago, the work of David Chandler carpenter who was at Ruperra castle about 44 years the first market (cart) that was used there was no springs cast.

April. 13th Cutting up the trees by the General's walk. *('The General' was Thomas Morgan of Ruperra, MP and Judge Advocate General (1702- 1769), father of Jane Morgan, the last of that particular branch of the Morgan line at the time. She married Sir Charles Gould who changed his name to Morgan to continue the line.)* My back is no better.

April 14th Heard the cuckoo today. *(Like all country people, then and now, he thought hearing the cuckoo was important.)*

May 4th Caught 19 lame ewes. Found a pheasant's nest. Finished tailing all the lambs. I hear that Tredegar ewes and lambs are looking very bad. They say the ewes are rotten. *(This seems to indicate some rivalry!)*

Home Farm Sheep and Lambs 2004

July 31st Mother gone to Rudry Mill to order meal and pay for the last. A very hot day 72 deg. in the shade. Cut down the Scotch Firs that died on the Green. Hauling water from the pond to Ruperra Garden. The Colonel been two days down to Tredegar Cricket match. *(The water shortage didn't inconvenience the Colonel too much it seems.)*

Aug 10th One of the milking cows got stuck in the bog in the Deer Park. *(This is the area of the large fields to the west of the castle, where deer sheds can still be seen. The Park is thought to be either medieval or to be the creation of Thomas Morgan when he built the castle in 1626.)*

Aug 15th The Colonel came back from Brecon. Up there 4 days after grouse.

Aug 16th Colonel went to the Carmarthenshire Show. Joe Spooner took his luggage to the station. *(See page 86. There were many Spooners working on the estate. Roy Hawkins, whose mother was a Spooner, remembers Granny Spooner sitting in her rocking chair, with her shawl round her shoulders. Joe lived in Parkwall at one time, kept the PO in Michaelstone at another and moved to the Draethen when he retired. Eli Spooner, whose parents, Daniel and Mary also lived at Parkwall, moved from Penhow Farm to Hillside in Rudry. His brother David (Dai, the pig butcher) lived at Ty Gawla Bach Farm on the Cefn Mably road. Another brother Edwin who was the terrier man with the Tredegar hounds, used to have his two terriers sat on the horse in front of him.)*

Granny Spooner had a hard life at Ty Gawla Bach

Aug 18th Finished harvesting. Mr and Mrs Hoare. *(Colonel Freddie's daughter Blanche and C T Hoare, a banker)* came to the Castle.
Mr Stratton, Machen Place sowed wheat and cut it and hauled it in 15 weeks. (*Richard Stratton, Tredegar farm manager and his family lived at Plas Machen from about 1880 to 1928. It had been the seat of the Morgans of Machen before they moved to Tredegar House in the 1660s. See the map)* This has been the finest summer I have ever seen I think in my life. In the summer of 1844 the first holly trees were planted in the drive. *(This is interesting information for garden historians. There are very few holly trees left today.)* In the year 1898 on August 16th *(Almost exactly a year previously)* it rained and thundered most awful. It was so dark we had to

light a candle to have our dinner. The Colonel won a prize at Carmarthen. The taps ran dry today. *(Did he mean the taps at the castle? Or did Home Farm have tapped water?)*

October 16th The war with the Transvaal is begun. Lord Tredegar sent 16 horses. *(Tenants' horses were bought from them by the Estate for the war.)*

October 17th Bassaleg Ploughing match held at Gwernleyshon. The Colonel could not stop for the dinner. Had to go to London for the opening of Parliament about the Transvaal war. Lord Tredegar was at the match.

Nov 21st Buried Fred Webb. Killed our pig today 20 score 8. Mr Rowlands the Mills Birthday. Lovely time there *(It's good to think of the Beecheys enjoying themselves with all their friends and neighbours at the party in the Mill.)*

Dec.6th The Colonel and Gentry all round here today. My finger very sore today. Had to poultice it. I cut it 9 days ago. *(There were no antibiotics until after the Second World War. You had to make sure that infections were kept under control.)*

1900

Jan 6th They say that Mr Courtney got to go out to South Africa. Tom Jones' cob is sold to Mr Stratton for South Africa.

August 6th Poaching this morning. 13 here from Risca. Had a bad row over it by the iron bridge. Ted Watts and Alfred Beacon and Reckless and a police team. *(These were game keepers on the Estate.)* Mr Reckless had a bad cut over the eye. They went to Risca after them. Mr Reckless could not walk home, came back in a trap.

August 7th The new cook came tonight. Mrs Jones. and a new kitchen maid. Took a sheep up to the castle 58 lbs and 36 eggs also bacon 52 lbs and a ham and 2 fowls. The kitchen and larders look clean. *(William was obviously interested to see whether the previous cook had been doing her work properly.)*

August 9th Dr Cullinham to Reckless.
Aug 22nd Reckless is getting about.

Aug 25th Poachers had to pay £80. *(This was a steep fine even when divided between them all. Compare with a labourer's pay of five shillings a week on the estate).*

Sept 9th Chapel Anniversary today. Three sermons. *(He doesn't say whether he enjoyed them or not.)*

Sept 29th Skinned a fawn. Done 5. Killed the old black ram out of the deer Park. He was the one that knocked Ann Davies down. Took him up to the castle. *(It must have taken some cooking to make him edible. Maybe the meat was used for the hunting dogs.)*

Oct 2nd Colonel returned to parliament unopposed. Went up to the castle to hear him speak. A lot of people up there singing and dancing. Been in parliament about 26 years. Colonel drove carriage and pair to Newport. A new carriage. That's more than I have seen for 40 years. *(Colonel Freddie didn't like spending money.)*

1901

Jan 22nd Queen Victoria died. Moved the foot rot tub out of the yard into the hay shed. *(Life must go on, even when a much loved Queen of 64 years' reign dies.)*

Jan 25th Beat today round the Preserve. Killed 81 rabbits 16 pheasants. Very stormy day. Jim Spring and boy cutting wood in the Graig. *(Coed Craig Ruperra to the north of the castle)*

Feb 2nd Buried the Queen today. Had a holiday. It was a universal one. Mr Reeves the minister had a memorial service in the afternoon

1902

Jan 15th Colonel up to Cwmbran spouting in answer to Alfred Thomas MP. He has been up there running the Colonel down. *(Alfred Thomas MP 1840-1927. Mayor of Cardiff in 1881, he represented the newly formed constituency of East Glamorgan from 1885–1910, being elected chairman of the Welsh Parliamentary Liberal Party in 1898. He was instrumental in setting up University College Cardiff and the first president of the National Museum of Wales. Elected president of the Welsh Baptist Union, he became*

Baron Pontypridd in 1912. *The changes in the social structure were becoming more obvious.)*

June 13th Finished shearing 224. Little Rowland sheared a little on two of them, tied them, pitched them and packed up the wool. *(William was proud of his children.)*

June 24th The King is very ill. Gone under operation. Coronation put off. Is as well as can be expected. Tis a tumour.

June 26th The King was not crowned. A sad disappointment. But we had our treat up at the schools. It was a lovely day and there was a good spread there for all.

Oct 13th Colonel ill again

Oct 24th Colonel down for meals in the dining room .

October 29th My birthday William Beechey 55 years

Oct 30th Colonel is better. Been all round here. Little Stradling came here to work. *(Either Arthur, 3 years older than Bert Stradling, or Bill, 7 years older.)*

Nov 20th Colonel out on horseback today .

Dec 4th Colonel and Miss Millar gone to Bath to try the waters for health *(Miss Millar is mentioned in the 1901 Census as a 'visitor'. In another part of the diary she is shown to have a position of authority in the Castle.)*

By 1918 William Beechey, still faithfully writing up his diary, paints a rather different picture of life at Ruperra. With the Morgans no longer in residence, the surplus of food was sent to Courtenay, Lord Tredegar, at Tredegar House. William now 72 years of age was not in very good health. He does seem to have recovered by the end of the year however.

1918

April 27th Mr McKinnon up to London to see his son Bert. *(Angus McKinnon, the head gardener, whose son Robert lost his arm in WWI.)*

August 23rd All the wheat now in. Garden party and ball at the Castle tonight. Fine night. Got the oil engine on the elevator.

August 25th prayer meeting all day
.

Oct 21st Heard that Rowland is coming home. *(Presumably from the war.)*

Nov 8th Pay today £8 12 *(Probably a monthly payment. A servant cooking and cleaning on the Ruperra estate in the 1920s got £3.12 a month. Does this mean that he must have had a higher postion than the shepherd of the 1901 census?)* The flu about very bad

Nov 11th The Armistice signed and peace.

Dec 1st Shoot at Ruperra today 164 pheasants.

Dec 3rd Germans come to Ruperra. Today 6 of them.

Dec 6th A meeting up at the school about the soldiers. wanted all the parish up there. Germans drawing swedes in New Georgy.

1919

July 25th and 26th Clearing the castle out all furniture. 6 loads gone from the castle. *(Possibly because of Courtenay's refurbishment of Ruperra.)*

Aug 2nd Will and Rosa and Lister came here tonight. We all had a walk around the Castle.

Aug 8th Presentation for Douglas McKinnon. *(The Head Gardener's son, commissioned officer in either the Royal Air Force or the Royal Flying Corps in the First World War.)*

Sept 10th Mrs Lindsay at the Castle in her car. *(Courtenay's sister married to Col. Lindsey of Ystrad Fawr, chief constable of Glamorgan. A car was unusual enough for a comment.)*

Sept 27th 78 Eggs for Tredegar House. Railmen all gone on strike.

Oct 4th the strike has been on 8 days. Sunday the day the strike came to an end.

Nov 3rd This is Lord Tredegar's show day. The first for 5 years owing to the War.

Nov 27th I was taken bad and was unable to go to London for Rowland's wedding. *(This must have been very upsetting for him and the family. However he was back to strength by the new year and his life back to normal)*

1920
Jan 2nd Killed our pig about 11 score. Fred Lewis at Tirzah. Caught all the lame ewes. Took the ewes to the Barn Field. 31 eggs to Tredegar.

William's grave in Tirzah Churchyard. His first wife Matilda's name is above his, and his second wife Ann's, below

CHAPTER FIVE RUNNING THE ESTATE

In 1901 the Ruperra Estate was in its heyday and the census returns for that year for the areas around Ruperra show many agricultural occupations. People from all the villages around would have worked on the estate. In Rudry and parts of Michaelstone some land was owned by the Cefn Mably, Bute and Plymouth estates but from Ruperra eastwards into Monmouthshire, and northwards as far as Tredegar itself, Tredegar ownership was very extensive.

William Beechey's diary shows that much of the day-to-day work on the Ruperra Estate was shared out amongst employees who could turn their hands to most things. The grounds, gardens and woodland had to be kept in good condition, herds and flocks had to be tended and food had to be produced for the family at the Castle, their visitors and those who looked after them. Many were local but others would hear about the availability of jobs from travelling salesmen for example in Pembrokeshire and Cornwall.

There was also the specially qualified staff in charge of the grounds, the gardens, the horses, the game rearing and the domestic work. Most of these came from other parts of the United Kingdom and were both sought after and seekers themselves and the estate was obviously a very good place to be employed. Only the best were employed at this stately home.

Some of the census returns for 1901 for the castle are printed on the next two pages. Census returns are fascinating to study and I recommend anyone who is interested, to go to the Record Offices to see the entries for the whole Ruperra Estate and the villages around. Apart from anything else it is interesting to note how much people moved about in those days.

Doris Oram, who as a child lived in Trescuthan, a little white cottage on the opposite side from Coed Ruperra on the Draethen-Michaelstone road, knew that as well as the locals 'there were people working on the estate from all over the place. Mr McKinnon, the head gardener was a Scotsman. The Raes at the Hollybush were also Scots. Mr Rae was head forester and in charge of all the woodsmen on the estate. Tom Pembridge, a very tall thin man, very reserved, was a proper Englishman. He was in charge of the horse and trap which had two benches in it. He also looked after and cleaned the harnesses of the horses, as well as helping in the gardens. He'd go to town to shop in the horse and cart for all the others and then later on he was a chauffeur. He sometimes drove the McKinnons about. And he was bearer for all the 'toffs' funerals like Mr Stedman of Machen House. His wife May, who came from Llandyssyl, was a bit on the busy side and 'nosy.''

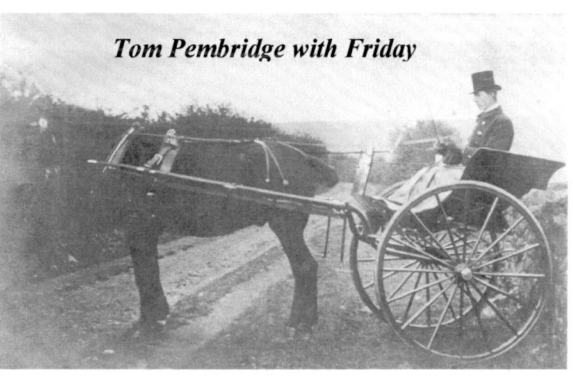

Tom Pembridge with Friday

Tom was well liked and a very useful man on the estate. Born in 1891, he died in 1978 at the age of 87. When the castle was requisitioned at the outbreak of war he was charged with keeping records of the quick succession of regiments that, even after the castle was burnt down, passed through their training there.

'Frank Godel, a Jersey man was a gardener and also did extra jobs around the castle.' *His granddaughter Edna, remembers her father Walter* 'going with him to stoke the boilers in the castle and they would gather mushrooms on the way.'

William Credgington from Bridgenorth in Shropshire was a carpenter on the estate. Like many others, his descendants stayed in the area and are still here today. Doris Oram talked about her own father Jack Squires, who was already there. 'He used to fetch the coal from Church Road Station in Lower Machen and take it down the drive to the Castle. He was a waggoner with the horses. That was all he did because they had two big shire carthorses delivering the coal from the station twice a day to keep the Castle going. I can remember once we were dressed nicely to go to school and we had a ride with my father in the waggon and when we got off my sister was fuming because our dresses were all dirty. She tried to clean mine by spitting on her hankie!'

As can be seen from the census returns, the employees came from a great variety of places, both the specialist ones like game keepers and grooms, and the more humble housemaids and farm workers. People certainly moved around in their search for jobs.

1901 Census Return for Ruperra Castle

Column 1 shows the number of the dwelling on the census.
Column 2 the road, street or name of house.
Column 3 the houses inhabited
Column 4 the number of rooms occupied if less than five
Column 5 the name and surname of each person.
Column 6 the relation of that person to the head of the family.
Column 7 the condition as to marriage
Column 8 the age of the person last birthday, divided into male and female

Please read across the two pages.

1	2	3	4	5	6	7	M	F
48	Ruperra Castle	1		Ivor Cosslett	Brother	S	39	
				Frederick C. Morgan	Head	Widr	66	
				Frederick G. Morgan	Son	M	27	
				Dorothy S. Morgan	Daur-in-law	M		22
				Ella K. Millar	Visitor	S		44
				Mai a M Morris	Visitor	S		23
				John J. Mills	Servant	S	41	
				Edward Sloggett	Serv	M	55	
				Daniel Rowntree	Serv	S	17	
				John T. Walters	Serv	S	22	
				Emily Windsor	serv	S		29
				Evaline M Ranger	serv	S		30
				Florence E. Rainger	serv	S		18
				Emma Bailey	serv	S		27
				Margaret A Jones	serv	S		26
				Edith R Watts	serv	S		25
				Elizabeth Williams	serv	S		21
				Elizabeth James	serv	S		17
				Hannah Meyrick	serv	S		21
				Annie Nicholas	serv	S		18
				Margaret E Evans	serv	S		17
Total of Schedules, of Houses and of Tenements with less than Five Rooms		3				Total of Males and of Females	12	18

Column 9 the profession or occupation
Column 10 whether the employer, worker or 'own account'
Column 11 whether working at home
Column 12 where born
Column 13 deaf and dumb, blind, lunatic, imbecile, or feeble minded.
Column 14 the language spoken

Carter on Farm			Monmouth, Castleton	Both
Member of Parliament	Employer		Sussex, Brighton	English
Squire, Living on own means			Glamorgan, Llanrwedo	English
			Do Cowbridge	English
			Wilts, Segray	English
			Carmarthen, Coomb	English
Butler	Domestic		Bedford, Leighton Bozzard	English
Valet	Do		Glamorgan, Llanidan	English
Footman	Do		Norfolk, Sall	English
Groom	Do		Carmarthen, Llanilloyd	Welsh
Cook	Dom Do		Brecon, Llangattock	English
Lady's maid	Do		Gloucester, Didbury	English
Do	Do		Do Do	English
Laundrymaid	Do		Mon. Monmouth	Welsh
Dairymaid	Do		Monmouth St Mellons	English
Housemaid	Do		Oxford, Fritwell	English
Do	Do		Pembroke, Killgerran	Both
Do	Do		Do Do	Both
Kitchenmaid	Do		Do Lampeter	English
Scullerymaid	Do		Glamorgan, Magor	Both
Laundrymaid	Do		Salop, Clun	English

The Census Return for a few of the other houses connected with the castle.

The column references are the same as on the previous page.

The office was probably the Bothy; the gamekeepers house, the Preserve: Ruperra Park refers to the four Parkwall cottages along the Ruperra Drive.

	Administrative County	Glamorgan					The undermentioned Hou...			
1901	Civil Parish of Llanvedw (Rhiwa)		Ecclesiastical Parish of Michaelston of Vedw (?)			County Borough, Municipal Borough, or Urban District		Ward of or of		
Cols 1	2	3	4	5	6	7	8	9	10	11	12
No. of Sch.	ROAD, STREET, &c., and No. or NAME of HOUSE	HOUSES Inhabited	Uninhabited In Occupation	Not in Occupation	Building	Number of Rooms if less than Five	Name and Surname of each Person	RELATION to Head of Family	Condition as to Marriage	Age last Birthday of Males / Females
49	The Office, Ruperra	1					Thomas John Edwards	Head	S	38
							Charles H. Brown	Boarder	S	24
							John Lewis	Boarder	S	18
50	Gamekeepers House	1				4	Philip Reckless	Head	M	52
							Dora E. Do	wife	M	59
							Clara E. Do	Daur	S	23
51	Ruperra Park	1					William a Thomas	Head	M	37
							Sarah Do	wife	M	38
							Edith K. Do	Daur		1
							Edward Watts	Boarder	S	21
							Zilpha Watts	Visitor	M	61
52	Ruperra Park	1				3	Thomas Morgan	Head	M	61
							Margery Morgan	wife	M	60
53	Ruperra Park	1				3	Joseph Spooner	Head	M	30
							Esther Do	wife	M	31
							Phillip D. Do	son		5
							Mary R. Do	Daur		3
54	Ruperra Park	1				4	George Lewis	Head	M	37
							Eliza Do	wife	M	36
							Walter Do	son		1

The headings along the top of these two pages refer to the details of the district of the census. First the Administrative County, Glamorgan, then the

Civil parish, Llanfedw, then the ecclesiastical parish Michaelstone y Fedw (part of) then the rural District, Llandaff and Dinas Powis, then the Parliamentary Division, Eastern Division, Glam and lastly the hamlet, Llanvedw.

Anyone wishing to look at the rest of the census will need to know the names of the County, the Civil and ecclesiastical Parish and the hamlet. I believe this particular census can be found on microfiche in Newport Reference Library, at Newport Record Office at the County Hall in Cwmbran and at the Glamorgan Record Office in Cardiff. It is as well to ring first to book a microfiche machine. Operation is not difficult and the archivists are very helpful.

PROFESSION OR OCCUPATION	Employer, Worker, or Own account	If Working at Home	WHERE BORN	(1) Deaf and Dumb (2) Blind (3) Lunatic (4) Imbecile, feeble-minded	LANGUAGE SPOKEN
Stud Groom	worker		Glamorgan, Neath		Both
Groom	worker		Gloucester, Clifton		English
Groom	worker		Glamorgan, Caerphilly		Both
Gamekeeper	worker		Notts, Hinxpton		English
			Worcester, Wolverly		English
			Leicester, Newton Linford		English
Coachman Domestic			Pembroke, Burton		English
			Oxon, Fritwell		English
			Glamorgan, Llanfedw		
Groom Domestic			Oxon, Fritwell		English
			Do Do		English
Stone Mason	worker		Monmouth, Michaelston y Fedw		Both
			Glamorgan, Llanvedw		Both
Groom Domestic			Do Drayclin		Both
			Monmouth, Michaelston y Fedw		Both
			Glamorgan, Llanvedw		English
			Do Do		English
Cattleman on Farm	worker		Monmouth, Michaelston y Fedw		English
			Kent, Chatham		English

There follow now some accounts of life at Ruperra in the first quarter of the 20th century, from individuals and their relations who worked on the Estate.

William Beechey mentioned 'Little Stradling' starting to work on the Estate on October 30th 1902. Little Stradling's brother Bert was to follow him, in 1906. Bert, who died in 1988 at the age of 96 said that he left school on the Friday and started work on the following Monday on his 14th birthday.

Bert's grandparents had lived in the Cwm Cottages in Rudry. The ruins can still be seen by the side of the fast flowing millstream along the Public Footpath from Rudry to Lisvane in the Cwm. On marriage, Bert's father moved to Ffald Gerrig. Bert remained convinced to the end of his life that he was descended from either an illegitimate branch of the Stradling family of the Vale of Glamorgan or from a disgraced member who had emigrated to France and never come back. He was never able to find the connection.

Bert's father died in 1900 when Bert was eight and from then on the family had to struggle. His eldest brother died in a mining accident. 'My father had been unconscious for three weeks after an accident in the colliery. He had got over that and had started a pony and trap oil business. He had a shed in the field down by the spring in the Cwm. *(The field and the gate are still there)* The pony was a bit on the flighty side and she pulled and went for the gate with the trap, as he was trying to put her in the field. The wheel went over his ankle. He'd only broken a small bone but he died the next day of shock He wasn't 50. My mother was a widow after that until she died when she was 92. She was always working - the 'Lloyd George' hadn't come in then - housework, chickens, making puddings from the pig brains, taking the oil cart round. We boys, there were five of us, had to do the

Bert as a young man

garden, grow vegetables. We all had to help in the house.

The west entrance of Ruperra Castle

Since I had a brother already working at Home Farm, I went down there with him and saw the bailiff and got taken on. I was a big man going to work that morning with my old straw frail on my back. I went over the field from Ffald Gerrig, over the stile onto the road and into Ruperra Park by those steps at the side of the black gate *(see the main map and the picture on the next page)* and along the drive to the Castle. We'd go inside through the back door *(west door)* and down a step. Right opposite was a stairs and the first flight went straight up to the Butler's pantry. We used to have a feed there on the quiet.

I was supposed to start work at 8 o clock but I always had to wait for the post boys to bring the post up to the Castle and then we used to sort it and I'd go off with mine to East Lodge on the Michaelstone Road and to the farm beyond. There was a lot of post because Colonel Freddie was MP for Monmouthshire. All

Gwern Leyshon Farm

the houses belonged to Tredegar. There were another two cottages at Llanvedw Farm and I used to take their milk tins and a tin from East Lodge and get their milk for them from the bailiff's farm. *(Mr Rymer at Gwern Leyshon)* I'd get back about 9 or 9.30, after a round trip of 3 miles and then I'd do jobs around the

Castle. I earned five shillings a week and was paid once a month at the end of the month.

Ruperra used to grow a lot of corn and stuff at the Home Farm. You'd see five or six horses working in the same field ploughing. I've seen a cabbage grow in a field in Ruperra in amongst the swedes, which weighed twenty-six pounds. They grew huge swedes and carrots for the horses by dropping seeds in with the crops.'

Bert was very interested in the estate walls. 'There were black gates or doors in the wall around the estate which were always kept locked except on hunting days. So nobody from outside could ride in there except on hunting days The estate workers who lived outside the estate, used the steps in the wall at the side of the doors to get to work. They looked after those doors and steps well. They used to tar them regularly.'

When Mary Thomas worked for the McKinnons in the Bothy in the Castle grounds, as we will see in the next chapter, she had to walk over the little bridge over the stream, from Cwm Leyshon Cottage and up through the woods, over the steps by the black door between Roy Hawkin's smallholding and West Lodge and onto the castle drive. (The steps are still there although a stile has been erected for the public footpath).

Steps on the side of the wall between Ty Cornel and Ty Gawla.

'The doors were pulled down by later owners,' *said Bert*, 'often leaving a gaping hole in the lovely walls, but the remains of the steps can sometimes be found. There's a new gate on the road from Ty Cornel to Ty Gawla where the wall is down but one pillar can be seen. There was a footpath going right inside the Castle grounds too and connecting with a paved path to the south gate of the Castle. After that it went across the field to the Cefn Mably road. *(The path now goes outside the Castle wall but nobody knows when it was diverted, if it ever was.)*

By the main gate going in to the Castle there was a two-stall stable on the corner where the stud groom kept the saddles. The colonel's best horses were kept there, Torpedo 11 and Schonbelle. He used to do a lot of racing, and always ran in the Ely races. The Colonel was a good horseman. If he wanted a long run they would open the gate into the field between the Preserve and the present day milking parlour and they'd go down to the bottom of that hill to where you can turn up to Ruperra and then go up to the top of the park to Ruperra Park Lodge. I can remember the ring of trees with a double fence around them and poles which could be highered or lowered to make a training circus. They used to do things in style! The head groom at the Castle was called Champion, probably the same family as the Grand National family. He went from here to a big racing school or estate in England.'

The Morgans were very keen sportsmen and huntsmen and a great deal of effort and expense was put in to making sure that the Ruperra Estate could provide good shooting and hunting. Janey Powell whose mother was Nettie (Janet) McKinnon, daughter of the Head Gardener and married to a Basham, could remember a day in the 1930s when the Bute family came up to visit.

'The Butes came hunting one day in their Rolls Royces, bringing very small

A postcard of Ruperra in the 1930s

children with them and all their people and their nannies and servants. They didn't stay at the Castle - they just came to hunt and they came in through the south gate not through the one on the drive that we came through. They rode their own horses and there were grooms there seeing to them.

I used to go cubbing with my brother. We used to park the car at the Hollybush and then we'd walk up towards the Castle and I'd be afraid to lose sight of him because I wouldn't know how to get home without him. He used to make me run down the hill from the summer house. I had a pad given to me, a fox's pad, but unfortunately I took it to have it cured and they lost it. And then my mother had a brush and she had it made into a fur thing with a big brown bow. I suppose it looked lovely but I felt really embarrassed having to wear it to church'

Bert Stradling had more to add about the hunting. 'Colonel Lindsay (*of Ystrad Fawr*) married to Colonel Freddy Morgan's daughter Blanche, was master of the Glamorgan hounds. They used to bring their horses right down to Rudry regularly and gallop over the mountain to Bedwas. The Colonel and his other daughter Violet, Mrs Munday used to hunt a lot as well. They were always out in front of all the others. She could ride and the old boy too. That's what ended his days. He'd stop in the saddle all day getting soaking wet and he had rheumatic then, poor old boy.'

Tommy Harris from Machen remembered Molyneux, the master of the Hounds. 'They hunted Tuesdays, Thursdays and Saturdays. They met in the Ffwrwm or the Old Machen Station. A big day out that was. The only day I'd mitch from School! I always remember Molyneux riding his horse down the steep escarpment from the summer house on Craig Ruperra and the horse's eyes showing he was frightened to death. But he had to go down. They'd hunt all over there.'

Kath Ayres had this to say about the fox hunting. 'Now I'm not a bit interested in fox hunting but I think when the foxes go to earth they should leave them. They shouldn't dig them out. In any case they don't catch many foxes round here, the foxes give them the run around. Now my mother's family and my father's family (except for my mother and father themselves) were all interested in hunting. They would leave their work – even if they were doing the washing they would leave that to go for an hour's hunting! I remember my grandmother taking me hunting one day. I was about eight. And they killed in front of the Castle in that field and she said she was disgusted with me because I turned green and I was sick in front of everybody! My mother said, "you ought to have more sense than to let her see a kill". I was a tough kid but that, I couldn't stand.'

Game keeping, and the shooting of the game of course were a very important part of the life of the Castle and also used to provide extra employment for many. Bert Stradling said that 'They used to rear about 4 thousand birds a year at Ruperra and they had a couple of very big shoots there. You could earn 5/- a day for beating and you'd have a pair of rabbits to come home. (Bert's job on the estate earned him 5/- a week) And if you could carry the cartridge bag for one of the 'toffs' who were shooting, he'd give you a tip. I always used to look out for J H T Brain of Brain's Brewery. There was always a £1 tip from him. Ruperra and Cefn Mably used to have a shoot one week after each other. If the birds were heading from one place to the other they'd let them go, ready for the next week but if they were flying away they'd take a shot at them.

The 'toffs' used to have their lunch at the Castle and we'd have ours in the Bothy where the gardeners were. We'd have a good feed; Mr McKinnon the Head Gardener would put a shovelful of onions in the ashes under the grate.

The Preserve

The under keepers used to come round the district buying up broody hens. You'd sell them your old ones and then buy them back afterwards for half the price. Sometimes you'd get good 'uns back in their place! They'd put the pheasants' eggs under the hens and each hen would hatch out about three lots of pheasants.'

The daughter of Mr Thomas the keeper from 1914 until the Blackburns came, wrote out an account of some of her father's work for the present day owners of the Preserve where the head keeper always lived. The set up there was purpose built for game keeping. The outbuildings consisted of the gun room, also a long open sided shed along side where the ferrets were kept in little boxes and a 'Dog House' where two or three retriever dogs were kept. While their house was scrubbed out each day, the dogs got up onto a table with straw under them. The broody hens, wrote Miss Thomas 'sat on about 14/15 eggs in nest boxes along the inside of the park wall. Each hen was taken off the nest every morning, a slip knot of string was put on the leg and fastened to a stake in the ground to give them sufficient freedom to walk about and have their food. After a period they were put back on their nests. When the chicks were old enough they were moved into hen coops with little runs in the big field in front of the castle. There was then a keeper in the field all day feeding them with hard boiled eggs chopped up and boiled rabbits put through a mincer.

As they got older they were let out to run in the field and what a job the keeper had getting them in to the old hens at night. Sometimes on a nice June summer evening it would be midnight before he got them off the field – and there was no overtime in those days.'

Map of 1875 showing the field in front of the castle (top left) the house and outbuildings (centre right) and the planted woods behind the house

Bert Stradling remembered seeing the ' little platforms where they put corn for them to eat when they were older and straw for them to scratch. When they were big enough they'd take them into the woods, still with these platforms so that they could keep feeding them.'

What a difference from the rearing methods on the big shooting estates today where the pheasants have to have their beaks bound so as not to attack each other in the intensive conditions in which they are kept. Since a shoot these days can bring in thousands of pounds a day, the owners are looking for maximum profitability

Miss Thomas reckoned that even at the beginning of the 20th century 'at the time of shooting each bird had cost up to £5. After a shoot before Christmas, all the station masters between Newport and Paddington had a brace each and each porter two rabbits.'

A local resident, Cissie Jones lived along the road to Rudry from Draethen in Dyffryn Tawel. The land belonged to the Earl of Plymouth but bordered the Ruperra Estate, and Cissie remembered the pheasants from Ruperra 'all over the road and in our garden after the kidney beans. In the autumn there wouldn't be any beans left on the sticks. And they'd come and feed with our chickens too.' 'But' *said Bert* 'you dared not touch them in those days. If you shot or killed one you'd be had. But there used to be telegraph wires low down and sometimes the pheasants flying across from the top woods to the bottom would knock into them and drop into the gardens. I remember shaking with fright in case I met somebody when I was carrying home a pheasant under my coat that had flown into these wires.'

Colin Anstey, from the well known farming family and living then at Rhyd–y-Gwern Farm, described the fear of falling foul of the keepers or the land agents on the estate. 'My brother Philip (*farming at Home Farm after William Beechey*) used to take me rabbiting up there with the keepers. We'd have two days to go shooting rabbits but you mustn't shoot the pheasants. I was only a young nipper so I didn't have a gun but I had to carry the rabbits. I remember once they shot 200 in one day. There were rabbits everywhere there. And they'd go underground, the dogs would mark them and the keepers would come along and dig them out.

One day we were right by the castle wall which runs along the back road, just walking along with some people in front and Philip said 'Colin, there's a pheasant here look, do you think I ought to despatch him?' 'Go on' I said 'they won't miss him'

The drive at the back of the castle

So he dropped his coat on this bird. But he had to screw her neck to kill her of course and as he did so some feathers came off and blew up over the wall. It was a chance in a million! A keeper, it was Blackburn, put his head over the wall and said 'Good morning.' Phillip was frightened to death. He thought he was going to lose the farm! But the keeper never told!'

Edna Merrett remembers seeing her Grandmother Godel, who lived at Yew Tree cottage, coming back up the steep garden path after shutting up the chickens for the night. 'Her apron was stuck right out in front of her and her hands were holding on tight to something under the apron. It was a pheasant which had gone into the chicken coop. My grandmother had taken her chance since it was in her own garden, and screwed the pheasant's neck but even so she was careful to hide it while bringing it back to the house. There was a lovely dinner the next day!'

Special measures, both in the employment of gamekeepers and of policemen, had to be taken to deal with the poaching to which the estate was inevitably a prey. Bert remembered 'a lot of poaching and at one time four policemen just for Ruperra. They were at Cwm Leyshon, the Retreat, Ironbridge and Cwrt y Cebydd (now Green yard) in Rudry. Ashton and Sam Evans were at Ironbridge. Tredegar paid half the cost of the police. It was a good arrangement. The Chief Constable of Glamorgan, Colonel Lindsey of Ystrad Fawr was Colonel Courtenay's brother-in-law.

A lot of poachers used to come from Ochrwyth, down over the railway line and across the bridge over the Caerphilly-Newport road. Then they used to get down into Park Wood. *(Between Lower Machen and Rhiwderin)* The roads weren't up to much. There were four or five keepers at Ruperra trying to catch them and they'd have a rough time with some of them. Alf Beacon was the only keeper that could go over to Ochrwyth. They respected him there and would even buy him a drink, because if there was a summons and a court case he used to say exactly what had happened. He never told a lot of lies like some. But one time Alf had a nasty bout on the top there by Llwyn Celyn. (*On the Lisvane road*) There were two or three keepers and the police after a poacher in there by the name of Carpenter, but it was Alf who dropped across him. The fellow's gun jammed or Alf would have been a dead 'un. Even so he hit Alf with the butt of the gun and damaged his arm for good, but Alf stuck to him and they rolled down from the top to where the others were. Exciting times!'

In 1918 Courtenay Morgan closed down the Hollybush Inn in Draethen. Some say it was because of 'immorality' either in the pub or in the fields around but it was more likely because it was a focus for the poachers who would wait in the 'Six o'clock' field between Rhyd y Gwern and Draethen for the Hollybush to open at 6 pm when they would plan their night's poaching. So Mr Rae the chief forester, was put to live there as an extra keeper. 'Those were the days when everything on the estate was kept in good order' *said John Phillips of Clearwell Farm. The inn was not reopened as a public house until after the Second World War.*

At Trescuthan, Doris Orum remembered that 'the miners didn't have much wages at the time and there was quite a lot of poaching going on. So they'd all be in the Hollybush until closing time and out they'd go to different places to poach. They knew where the keepers would be. My father-in-law was a keeper over Rhiwderin way, Walter Head lived in a Parkwall cottage and Alf Beacon in Primrose Cottage *(set back on the right on the road to Rudry from Draethen.)* When I was about 15 or 16, I used to go and sit with Mrs Blackburn while her husband the Head Keeper was out watching for poachers in the night. Then when Mr Blackburn came back around midnight he would bring me as far as the Castle - you'd hear the clock chiming. I wasn't a bit afraid. I used to come on the ride with my brother's two Labradors and my mother used to come out on the door at Tresguthan with the lamp, because we didn't have electricity in those days, and I used to know she was there. As I'd come through the woods I'd see a cigarette here and there where the poachers were hiding. But I was never afraid. Its funny you could go out in those days and you weren't a bit afraid.

Kath Ayres remembered that 'everybody round here was employed on the estate. In my own family, my grandmother was head laundry maid at the Castle and her sister was next in line to her, so when my grandmother married my grandfather, her sister took the job over. So I had had two people in there. But you always gave up when you married. My grandfather was Edwin Jones, a blacksmith with the Ruperra Estate in the 20's. And I can never remember him swearing. Then when they started generating their own electricity in the castle, he used to run the generator. He also used to go down the park towards Cefn Mably to regulate the water in a box in the stream. I used to spend days with him in the summer holidays, taking sandwiches with me and they were rough and all!

The south west corner of the parkland

He was friendly with the head gardener Mr McKinnon and so I would go round the gardens and the glass houses and see the tomatoes and the peaches growing and all the beautiful flowers. In the gardens were all the vegetables you could think of to keep the Castle going. And there were free bags of manure off the farm for the estate workers.

When my grandfather retired he used to make faggots for Tredegar House and he'd get 5d or 6d for 2 or 3 dozen. They'd bring the wood to him, mind, it was all lovely and dry, like the feathery bits of birch, you know and he'd chop and tie them up And when he didn't have room for any more, they'd send a man up to pick them up on a lorry and take them down to Tredegar House for the fires down there, because there was no one at Ruperra then.'

Joe Spooner, when he retired, used to make brushes out of birch. Materials nor labour were ever wasted. In the 50s even, Jim Clifford would go from Michaelstone with his father to cut and bundle bean sticks in Coed Ruperra. 'You were paid for your work and then the bundles were sold on.'

Jeannie Wilson, the daughter of keeper William Greenway at the Preserve, remembered her grandmother, who lived at Holly House Cottage and repaired all the linen and fine lace from the Castle, describing earlier days when all the servants standing at the doors of their cottages in clean starched aprons, would dip a curtsey when the Morgan family went by in a pony and trap

Elwyn Edwards remembers Ivor Coslett living at East Lodge in the 30s. 'My grandmother Beechey adopted him and brought him up at the Home Farm. He was a very hard worker and was known for trimming the holly trees along the drive from Home Farm to the Castle. As there was no piped water at East Lodge, Ivor would carry two buckets on a yoke from the little well. He attended chapel in Castleton and was run over and killed, poor thing, in the black out in World War Two. *In charge of all the trimming and the thatching of hay and corn ricks on the estate was Jim Spring living by the bridge in Michaelstone.*

When Evan succeeded Courtnenay as Lord Tredegar in 1934, Morgan family visits to Ruperra became less frequent. To the long serving workers still in charge it must have seemed strange after the activity of previous years. Possibly, in their old age, the slowing pace of things didn't bother them too much, but they must have been aware that it was the end of an era. When the soldiers came in 1939 they still had roles to play, Tom Pembridge keeping records and maintaining the generators in good order, and Reg Blackburn repelling invaders – children picking flowers mostly- although perhaps those are the only incidents that people talk about. But Angus McKinnon, the head gardener, although a caretaker after his retirement, had died in 1935 a year after his wife of 52 years. So he never saw the castle burn down in 1941 or the neglect of his lovely gardens.

CHAPTER SIX ANGUS AND AGNES MCKINNON

Angus McKinnon was head gardener at Ruperra from 1894 to 1932. He was very well liked and almost as important to the estate workers as the Morgans themselves, particularly after the death of Colonel Freddie in 1909 when there were no more Morgans in permanent residence at Ruperra. He and Agnes his wife were very highly regarded by all who knew them and according to documented records he had gardened in prestigious places before becoming head gardener at Ruperra.

According to Peter Kerr, a relation of other McKinnons in Scotland, 'Angus was born in Appin, the son of Charles McKinnon of Morvern on Loch Linne. Some McKinnons had come over to the Scottish mainland in the 17th century and were eking out a farming existence in Morvern. Angus' grandfather, also named Angus, farmed at a place called Garbh Shlios, which is little more than a wild mountainside, falling steeply down to the sea. How they survived and fed their large family is a mystery. In 1841 Angus senior was

Angus and Agnes

Garbh Schlios
McKinnon's Bay

The house, now in ruins, was on a platform, (bottom right) with a little stream running by.

a charcoal burner. In the place still known as MacKinnon's Bay, oakwoods surrounded his house. Charles, his son was described in census returns as a land steward and sometimes a gardener. The McKinnons were hardworking and tough.'

Frimley Manor

Frimley great house the seat of Mr Tickell   Hassell 1822

By 1881 our Ruperra Angus had become head foreman at Falkland Palace in Fife. At the age of twenty three in 1882 he was married to Agnes Dobbie in Logie, Perthshire in the Church of Scotland, when he appears to have become a gardener at Frimley Manor Park in Surrey. The gardens of this manor had been laid by John D. Craig, also from Perthshire and at one time head gardener to the famous Sir Joseph Paxton. Had Angus heard of John Craig, who had at one time also been in charge of part of the grounds of the Crystal Palace? At any rate the job at Frimley was good experience for a young gardener and Angus may have brought to Ruperra some of the ideas of John Craig. Special mention is made in a sale catalogue for Frimley Park Estate in 1918, of "ornamental woodlands, intersected by remarkably fine Rhododendron walks"; a foretaste perhaps of the rhododendrons along the Ruperra Drive.

Ann Kerr née McKinnon

Angus' eldest son Charles was born at East Woodhay, Hampshire, the parish where Hollington House, now a luxury hotel, and Hollington Gardens, now open to the public, are situated. Perhaps Angus worked there before going to Rookery Hall in Cheshire where his daughter Janet was born in 1886 and where he was gardener for five years to Baron Schroeder.

Other members of the McKinnon family had worked at Rookery Hall at an earlier time, including one Ann McKinnon. In

1873 Ann had married James Kerr a tailor, who was another diary keeper. James' diary ran from 1879 to 1904 and contains some references to Angus McKinnon.

1885 "Mr McKinnon, Gardener, Rookery was with us for a short time."
May 1886: "Mr McKinnon, Rookery, brought ivy and stocks of rhododendrons which we planted this evening."
September 1903: "Mr McKinnon from Rupper (sic) Castle, Newport, Mon, came here tonight...
12 August 1904: "Ann and self to meet Mr McKinnon's of Lower Machen, Newport, daughter going through to Stirling. McKinnon sent with her a quantity of cut flowers for us."
"A McKinnon, Gardener, Ruppera Castle, Newport, Mon. left here today."

Ann Kerr's great grandson, Peter thinks "they must have had a well-disciplined upbringing. They frequently remind me of the tradition of the "Scotch Gardener" as typified perhaps by Mr McGregor in Beatrix Potter. I feel quite proud of my Highland ancestors."

Angus and family had moved to Lower Machen by 1891 where Angus was gardener to Mr W E Heard JP at Machen House. By 1894 Angus had been snapped up by Colonel Freddie Morgan to become head gardener at Ruperra at the age of 35. This was the pinnacle of Angus' career and he remained there until he died, totally dedicated to his job. Since his career coincided with the refurbishments carried out at Ruperra in the early part of the 20th century, his life must have been fulfilling and rewarding.

Angus McKinnon's grandson, another Angus was the son of John (Jack) the second son. He remembered going to stay at Ruperra as a little boy. It must have been about 1931, when his grandparents wee fairly old. He said

'Angus lived in Lower Machen in Parkfield House opposite the Church for ten years before he moved to the house next to the Castle where I went with my mother once; I think one of them was pretty ill and my mother had to go and look after them and I being so young and small had to be taken along. I seem to remember running round the garden but without my brothers and sisters there was nothing to do really except look out of the window there.

The McKinnon family just before World War I. From left to right, Janie, Robert, Janet, Angus, Charlie, Agnes, Mary, Jack and Douglas in the front

The only excitement for me down there was seeing them go off to church one Sunday morning in the pony and trap, and him all togged up in a top hat and grey striped trousers. Of course he was the head gardener and very prim and proper. They had fox hounds there, but I didn't see any of those.

Solitaire was a great game of theirs, which they used to play every night. In fact they showed me how to play it and I played it just like them! You would start and finish with a certain hole and it was the same every time!

In those days of course there was no television only radio and there used to be a charity appeal every Sunday night. Angus was old enough by that time to receive a state pension which was ten bob, but they didn't need it so they used to send it off to whatever appeal was on.'

Angus, Agnes and Robert

Mrs Janey Powell, daughter of Nettie (Janet) McKinnon, another grandchild, also remembered going to visit the McKinnons at Ruperra as a young child. "Robert McKinnon used to come down from London to my house and say 'come on let's go to Ruperra.' He'd lost his arm in the war and he used to do everything with the help of his teeth. - tie his tie and play cards. He was very smart and quick.

We'd go to Draethen on the bus, sometimes an open top bus in the summer, then walk up the side of the Hollybush, up over the top and go into the house where the McKinnons lived and we would stay a little while. While they were chatting they would send me out into the garden because I was only young. My grandfather used to say 'Help yourself' so I used to have strawberries. He had a wonderful eucalyptus tree which was his joy. Then we'd go and have a cup of tea and then occasionally, very occasionally, he would take me into the Castle and that was very exciting, because although he was a very brusque man he was very proud of it all.

Once a week they used to go shopping in Newport in the little horse and trap. He would drive it himself and the two of them would sit there with her dressed all in black and him with his slouch hat. As a little girl I thought they were very aloof people and we had to behave ourselves. In their house they had all these great big heating pipes for drying the hunting clothes, all the riding habits and things. *(Is this why some people call the Bothy the 'Laundry'? Or was it*

Angus and Agnes going shopping

because the bedlinen from the castle was washed there in the gardener boys' side, by Mary Thomas under the supervision of Agnes McKinnon.? Bothy seems a more suitable name for a head gardener's house.)

Janey continues. 'Their children were grown up and had all left home of course when I went there, so the two of them must have lived in the whole house. I didn't see any gardeners either - they had probably gone home for the weekend since usually it was a Sunday when I went. But it was all spotlessly clean.'

The impression that the grandparents made on these two children somehow is not quite the same as that of a newspaper report of 1935 describing Angus as a 'familiar figure at the Tredegar House Servants' Ball, where his jocular manner makes him a friend of everybody !' *The same report mentions that Angus had been responsible for carrying out Godfrey, Lord Tredegar's wishes regarding some fir trees which he had seen at Cheltenham and wanted to have as a feature in Ruperra Park. Angus had supervised the planting of the saplings. Angus' pride in his gardens and grounds was also reported.*

Marion Beeston whose family has lived in Lower Machen for generations and

The gardening staff in the 30s. Second left is Morris Jenkins, father of Edna Dix and third left in the front is Frank Godel with Billy Lloyd in the centre.

attended church there, remembers that St Michael's Church would be full on a Sunday. The servants from the castle would be there and the farmers from the surrounding farms had their own pews. The McKinnons too had their own pew; Angus was a church warden as well and greatly respected. Bert Stradling remembered that there were four or five gardeners under Mr. McKinnon. It seems they had increased in number by the 1930s. When Bert worked on the estate he remembered 'Jim Spring who lived by the bridge in Michaelstone. There was Wally Griffiths and old man Wheeley, a little bloke who used to keep the Castle kitchen supplied and would have his basket going around the garden, gathering up the vegetables every day. McKinnon was a good old stick. If I'd go in the garden, he'd come along and have a chat and he'd raise up the strawberry nets and say 'Go in under there and help yourself. A good old stick, old Mac.'

Elwyn Edwards remembered his mother telling him that when she lived at Home Farm and the lawns were cut in front of the castle the gardener put huge leather shoes on the horses' hooves so that they wouldn't damage the turf. South of the castle there were no flower beds just all lawns.

Leather shoes for horses

It is impossible however to talk about the McKinnons without mentioning Mary Thomas. Mary whose family lived at Cwm Leyshon Cottage, worked at Ruperra from 1920 when she was twenty, until 1933. Her job was to cook and clean for the gardener boys in the Bothy, so she knew the McKinnons well. Mary is on the far right.,

The Thomas Family

'I used to work in my Auntie Matty's little cottage *(Parkwall)* under Ruperra; I'd go up there to clean her kitchen on a

70

Saturday morning and Mr. McKinnon used to come across *(along the Ruperra Drive)* and bring the morning sticks for the week and veg more than likely and auntie would give him this hot beer. Mrs Lloyd had been housekeeper in the Bothy but she had died. I was only a young girl then so Mam took me up to the Bothy and they started me off there. It was a good position for me.

The Bothy is on the right of the picture. The McKinnons lived on the right of the archway. Angus is seen here feeding his chickens. The new stable block, built in 1905 to replace the one destroyed by fire in 1895 is on the left of the picture.

In 1910 the McKinnons had moved from Park Field House in Lower Machen and lived in the Bothy next to Ruperra Castle. On the left hand side of the arch lived the chauffeurs, the gardeners and apprentice gardeners. My job was to cook and clean for the gardener boys

In the Bothy I'd have to scrub the big room out and the huge big long table. I'd scrub it lovely and white. There was always a cloth to put on it. I used to lay it ready for their tea. The boys would come in from the garden then and put the gramophone on and start dancing and make a mess. And so I'd have to scrub the table over again after dinner because the boss, Mrs McKinnon, made sure that you did everything right. She was afraid in her heart for you to be idle a minute! Then I'd boil the water on the fire, and wash up all the dishes. The boys used to throw the cups and the plates to each other, amusing themselves! Then I could come home. On a Saturday I'd finish at one o'clock and then go back up on a Monday morning.

There was new accommodation in the Bothy for the chauffeurs but they stayed down in Tredegar House mostly because no-one had a car in Ruperra when I started there. The first one was an old Ford There was a posh wedding in Lower Machen and we all went and when Mr McKinnon and his wife turned up in this Ford you ought to have heard the crowds shouting 'Hurray!'

Anyway, whatever Mr McKinnon had in the garden he used to give me some of it to bring home. In the Spring he used to give my father seed potatoes and things like that. He always had yellow and red tomatoes in the greenhouses and the yellow were gorgeous. There were peaches, dates and figs growing outside against the wall and an orchard between the castle and West Lodge. After Mam died he'd always give me flowers to take to the churchyard. He was a nice person.

Mind, it was hard work for me. As well as my work for the gardener boys I used to have to clean *her* place, her range and my own. Those ranges were hard work! I'd have to clear out the ashes everyday of course and I used to clear out the flues with a scraper and a brush to get the soot out. I'd black lead them once a week. There'd be a block of black lead which you'd break up in a plate or something and mix with a few drops of vinegar There was nothing easy about it.

The McKinnons were typically Scots. And she was a one! As if I didn't have enough to do, I had to wash for her as well! And if the weather wasn't too good on a Monday morning you had to take the clothes right out on the green behind the Bothy. Sometimes she'd come over to the kitchen and say 'Mary, I think it's going to open up,' meaning that I should go and hang the washing out. And the boys would say 'Don't be so soft. It's your dinner hour, sit down! But of course you dared not do that. And she used to wear open drawers and when they were pegged out and the wind blowing through them the boys used to make fun and say 'Look at Mother's drawers!'

One time when I had done something wrong or forgotten to do something in the Bothy, she must have come and told me off good and proper! I came home and I told Mam that I couldn't stick it any more. I was off work for weeks anyway with gland trouble and I was worn out. She wanted an awful lot. Anyway Mr McKinnon came and begged me to go back because she 'took some understanding' he said and 'Mary understands Mother'. So I went back. It was supposed to be a good job. The girls about today, they don't know they're born.

The time I was ill Gwyn Lewis had to take over my job. Poor old Gwyn told me that on a Sunday morning when she used to go to Lower Machen Church, she couldn't listen to the vicar because she was thinking about washing Mr McKinnon's shirts on the Monday morning! He never rolled the sleeves of his shirt up and the stains of the tomatoes were terrible. Mrs Mac would say 'More elbow grease on those next week.' You were only allowed to use Hudson's washing powder and there was nothing in it. You'd rub the skin off your hands washing the clothes. Mrs Miles who came to help on a Saturday morning once hid some soda in her pocket to wash the shirts. She took her handkerchief out and the soda fell out! Of course Mrs McKinnon was standing by her and wanted to know what she wanted that soda for!

Mind she used to make soup for us and bring a basin over on a Tuesday with curly veg and parsley and not a veg out of it. I've never tasted anything like it. She'd make beautiful cake, bar yeast loaf and a sultana loaf all butter.

They used to keep bees and you'd have a square of the comb for your tea. They'd ask me to stop for tea sometimes and they'd send some things down to our house. And chickens, the way she used to cook the chickens, hens about a 12 months old,

Outside the Bothy

wrapped up in greaseproof paper then and put in a big saucepan and steamed with onions.

But you had to do things thoroughly. She wouldn't have anything half done. You had to get in the 'corrrners' as she used to say. On the day of her funeral one of the other girls said to me when we were sitting down quietly in Church 'What would Mother Mac say to see us sitting about, even on the day of her funeral!

I had been sitting by the table talking with her when she had the stroke. She was in her 70s. I looked after Mr McKinnon for a bit then, but he had a housekeeper as well and Ruth Richard's brother used to sleep there in the night.

Then one day, after I'd left Ruperra, Mary Stedman, Sir Foster Stedman's

Angus McKinnon's famous gardens

wife from Machen House, met my sister Enid along the road and said that Mr McKinnon had cancer and thought it right that I should know. And Mrs Rae, the forester's wife in the Hollybush said I should go and see him because he was so ill. So I went a few times to see him in the Royal Gwent Hospital.

When he saw me first, he cried and cried and the Sister tried to stop him by saying that I had come a long way to see him 'Ah! I can't hide it' he said. Ruperra meant so much to him and seeing me had brought it all back to him. People used to say that Ruperra could never go on without Mr. McKinnon. He worshipped it. Even when he went on holiday to Leicester he used to think about it all the time and imagine he could see the Channel. He was a lovely man.

And Evan Morgan never said he was sorry when Mrs McKinnon died in 1934. He was awfully upset about that because if it had been Evan Morgan's father it would have been different. Courtenay Morgan would go in and have a cup of tea with them at the Bothy. And he'd walk around the gardens with Mr McKinnon and both of them would sit on the front steps to talk.'

Angus and Agnes had celebrated their Golden Wedding in 1932 in Tredegar House. Newspaper reports in the Western Mail and the South Wales Argus and the list of subscribers in the Presentation Book, all testify to the great esteem in which they were held. Courtenay, Lord Tredegar and his son Evan sent letters and gifts. Evan's card accompanied a gold loving cup.

A gold Loving Cup was sent with the above visiting card.

A list of Subscribers to the Presentation to M͏r and M͏rs Angus McKinnon from the Tredegar Estate Agents Staff and Employees on the occasion of their Golden Wedding on 20th July 1932.

Tredegar Office staff	Tredegar Gardens
L. Foster Stedman	A. G. Allen
J. I. Storrar	O. Seyama
Major B. D. Corbet	C. Hazell
	A. Jones
J. F. Groves	J. Richards
W. B. T. Rees	J. Coslett
D. R. W. Derry	J. Hinder
F. A. Carter	D. Pembridge
J. C. Evans	R. Doody
E. Mowbray	A. Roberts
R. B. Moore	T. Hawkins
A. E. Petty	M. A. Bevan
F. Flanders	C. Davis
H. Daniels	G. Rees
Miss O. D. Barefoot	A. Perrott
Miss E. Williams	J. Buchanan

Tredegar Park	Tredegar Park (cont.)
Mr & Mrs T. Hillier	F. Buchanan
C. J. Williams	H. F. Evans
J. Marsh	W. Barrett
J. Evans	E. Blake
F. Sloman	W. Watkinson
W. J. Coleman	F. Richards
Mrs M. Williams	T. Heely
Miss R. Dooner	E. Western
J. F. Barnes	R. Gregory
F. Lambourne	J. Evans
O. Nicholls	W. Sayzeland
C. A. Barrett	J. Vaughan
A. Rees	T. Hazell

Tredegar Estate Works

A. C. Harding
W. Morris
E. Hodgkiss
C. Rowlands
J. H. Beeston
E. Marsh
D. Watson
W. E. Lewis
J. Jones
J. Dawson
A. E. Osmond
E. J. Jones
I. Jones
H. Phillips
W. Rees
D. R. Stinchcombe
S. T. Lewis

Tredegar Estate Works (cont.)

S. C. Harris
J. A. Gilford
S. J. Orders
E. Thomas
E. D. James
C. Vaughan
A. E. Lewis
J. James
N. C. Rees
A. Sabin
A. Taylor
D. Bishop
T. Jones
B. Gilford
I. Saunders
E. Lewis

Ruperra Castle

T. J. Pembridge
F. Godel
T. Beechey
M. Jenkins
Sgt. Smith
Miss M. Thoma.
Mrs Miles

Ruperra Engineers

Mr & Mrs G. W. King
J. Locke
W. Harding
T. Richards
F. Barrett
D. Harding

Ruperra Keepers

D. Holloway
D. Watson
H. Blackburn
A. Oram
A. Oram
C. E. Spooner
W. Head

Ruperra Woodmen

L. S. Rae
A. O. Morgan
A. Cox
J. Spring
J. Davies
T. Morgan
J. Richards
A. Thomas
A. Ellis
W. Western
J. Spooner
A. Crisp
R. Davies
H. Price

In the Presentation Book, there were pages of people sending their congratulations, which include some well known names.

Mr. & Mrs. E.G. Arnold.
Mr. W. Arnold.
Miss Baker.
Mr. J. & Miss Basham.
Mr. & Mrs. Blackburn.
Mr. & Mrs. Bliss.
Mr. & Mrs. Boucher & family.
Mr. & Mrs. F.S. Daniels.
Rev. S.M. & Mrs. Davies.
Dr. Edith M. Davies.
Misses M. & H. Dobbie.

Miss Ruttledge.
Mr. Rymer & family.
Mrs. F. Shaw.
Miss G. Shaw.
Mr. & Mrs. L. Foster Stedman.
Mr. & Mrs. F. Stratton & family.
Mr. R. Stratton. (The Duffryn)
Mr. & Mrs. E.G. Taylor.
Mr. & Mrs. D. Thomas.
Mr. & Mrs. Wade & family.
Dr. & Mrs. Wakeley.

Rev. D. & Mrs. Dudlyke.
Mr. & Mrs. Duff & family.
Mrs. Dunbar & family.
Rev. H. & Mrs. Evans.
Segt. J. & Mrs. Evans.
Mr. & Mrs. W.J. Evans & family.
Family :- Charlie; Nettie, Harry & Angus;
   Jack, Flo & Angus; Bert, Winnie & Jean;
   Douglas, Marie, & José & Sheila.
Mr. & Mrs. Gerrish.
Mr. & Mrs. R.D. Giles.

Mrs. M. Graham.
Capt. & Mrs. Griffiths.
Miss Alice Heard.
Mr. A. Heard.
Mr. M. Heard.
Mrs. M. Horn & family.
Mr. W.A. Hunt.
Mr. & Mrs. F. James.
Mr. H. Jenkins.
Mr. R.E. Jones.

Mr. A. & Miss Langmead.
Mrs. A. Lewis.
Mr. & Mrs. Locke.
Mrs. Mackay.
Miss Catherine McKinnon.
Mr. J. Moses.
Patrick Munro, M.P.
Mr. H. Murray.
Mrs. Peacock.
Mr. & Mrs. Perry.
Mr. & Mrs. Petty.

The Rector of Machen & Miss Picton.
Miss Pinchin.
Mr. & Mrs. Pinnell & family.
Miss Price.
Mr. P. Price.
Mr. & Mrs. Phelps.
Mr. & Mrs. Rae.
Rev. J. M. Raymond.
Mr. & Miss Rees.
Mr. R. E. Robb & family.
Miss J. Robb.

Sir Leolin & Lady Walker.
Mr. J. Williams.
Mr. H. Wylde.
Mr. B. Sinfield.
Mr. A. Fraser.
John Morgan Esqre.
Mrs. B. D. Corbet.
Rev. G. Picton.
Mrs. Hoare. The Honble
Dr. & Mrs. E. Llewellyn.
Mr. Roeyn Jones.
Corisande Lady Rodney

Copy of
Letter received from the Rt Hon. Viscount Tredegar.

Tredegar Park,
Newport
Monmouthshire
10th July 1951.

Dear McKinnon,

I understand that you and Mrs. McKinnon celebrate your Golden Wedding on Wednesday next, and I am anxious to be amongst the first to send you my most hearty congratulations.

You have spent a long, honourable, and I am sure happy life together, and I hope you may both be spared to one another for many years yet.

I enclose a cheque, which I hope you will accept with my best wishes, to be used in whatever way you may think best.

Believe me,
Yours sincerely,
Tredegar.

Reports from the Western Mail on the occasion of the McKinnon's Golden Wedding.

A LIFE SPENT AMONG THE FLOWERS.

GOLDEN WEDDING OF GARDENER.

Mr. Angus McKinnon, who has been head gardener at Ruperra Castle for the past 38 years, celebrates his golden wedding to-day.

Seventy-five years old and a native of Argyllshire, Mr. McKinnon for five years was gardener to the late Baron Schroeder at Nantwich, Cheshire, and then he came to Monmouthshire as gardener to Mr. W. E. Heard, J.P., at Machen House.

On October 1, 1894, Mr. McKinnon was appointed head gardener at Ruperra Castle by the late Hon. F. C. Morgan, father of the present Viscount Tredegar, and there he still is, held in great regard. Mr. McKinnon followed the late Mr. James Jones, who had been head gardener for 40 years and had succeeded his father who had held the post for 45 years. Thus Ruperra Castle has had three head gardeners in 123 years.

"Western Mail," July 20th, 1932.

GOLDEN WEDDING TRIBUTE

To Ruperra Castle Gardener and His Wife.

Mr. Angus McKinnon, head gardener at Ruperra Castle for the past 38 years, and his wife, who celebrated their golden wedding on Wednesday, were guests of the tenants of the Tredegar Estate.

A representative deputation waited upon them during the afternoon and on behalf of Mr. McKinnon's fellow-servants and the estate staff, presented him with a gold demi-hunter watch, and Mrs. McKinnon with a pearl and sapphire cluster brooch.

Mr. L. Foster Stedman, agricultural agent to the estate, made the presentations and paid tribute to Mr. McKinnon's loyal service over so long a period and to his high character. Others who spoke were Mr. J. I. Storrar (town and urban agent), Mr. J. F. Groves (estate architect), Mr. W. B. T. Rees (estate surveyor), Mr. F. Sloman (Tredegar House steward), Mr. A. C. Harding (estate clerk of the works), and Mr. G. W. King (estate electrician).

Among those present were Miss Helen Dobbie (Mrs. McKinnon's sister, who was a bridesmaid at the wedding), Mr. J. McKinnon (son), Mr. and Mrs. Bert McKinnon (son and daughter-in-law), and Mr. and Mrs. Harry Basham (son-in-law and daughter).

"Western Mail," July, 21st, 1932.

FLOWER SHOW FOUNDER.

Mr. McKinnon was the founder, with Mrs. C. T. Griffiths, wife of the late Dean of Llandaff, who was then rector of Machen, of the Machen Flower Show, which became one of the best shows in the country. He has judged all over the United Kingdom and has been one of the most regular judges at the great Bedwellty Show.

Mrs. McKinnon was Miss Agnes Elizabeth Dobbie, and the marriage took place in her father's house at Logie, Stirlingshire. There have been seven children. All four sons served in the war, and one lost an arm. Two had commissions. Of the three daughters only one survives. Mrs. McKinnon is two years younger than her husband.

Angus McKinnon is buried in the Churchyard of St Michael and All Angels in Lower Machen with his wife and two daughters who had died in 1916 when they were only 26 and 21. Agnes died aged 74 in August 1934 and Angus aged 77 in May 1935.

LATE MR. A. McKINNON, RUPERRA

Mr. Angus McKinnon, who was head gardener at Ruperra Castle for 40 years, was buried in Lower Machen Churchyard on Tuesday.

The Rev. F. A. Oswell (rector) officiated, assisted by the Revs. S. M. Davies (vicar of Rumney) and T. G. King.

Principal mourners were:—Messrs. Robert and Jack McKinnon (sons), Harry Basham (son-in-law), and Master Angus Basham (grandson).

Viscount Tredegar was represented by Mr. L. Foster Stedman, J.P. The following past and present Tredegar Estate employés attended:— Messrs. A, G. Allen (head gardener at Tredegar House), P. Holloway (head gamekeeper), C. Barrett, C. Williams, T. Hillier, Chepstow; A. Oram, J. Squires E. Jones, R. Young, Ruperra; A. Beacon, Ruperra; F. Roan, R. Greggory, F. North, J Evans, F. Lamborne, W. Price, G. W. King, W. J. Harber, H. Kelly, W. A. Knight, T. E. Beechey, W. Beechey, Bowen Rees, P. Perry, and F. F. Flanders.

Others present were:—Mr. C. J. Forestier-Walker (representing Mrs. Charles Forestier-Walker), Lady Forestier-Walker, Mrs. Griffiths, the Rev. D. Dudlyke, Tredunnock; Mrs. L. Foster Stedman, Mr. E. L. Melville Heard and Miss Heard (representing Mr. W. E. Heard, J.P.), the Rev. D. Evan Thomas, Newbridge; Mr. Charles Basham (chairman, Bedwellty Show), the Rev. D. R. Jones, Rudry; Mr. and Mrs. Ivor Thomas, Messrs. E. Hardinge, Rumney; H. Merrett, Llanrumney; J. Gimblett, I. Everson, E. John, W. H. Palmer, John Davies, D. T. Newton Wade, J. Ashton, W. Kite, Castleton; T. Davies, G. R. Beeston, H. Matthews, F. Stratton, T. Richards, the Rev. A. G. A. Picton (vicar of Bassaleg), Capt. W. T. Harris, Messrs. Grosvenor Harris, W. J. Evans, Stanley Evans, Harry Jenkins, Barry; John Duff, Tredunnock; J. Wattie, and Reg. James.

Funeral arrangements were carried out by Arthur Burleigh, Newport.

The inscription on the gravestone reads simply "ANGUS MCKINNON OF RUPERRA CASTLE GARDENS

CHAPTER SEVEN   A LITTLE GIRL'S STORY

Perhaps it was the tragic death of Angus McKinnon's two daughters that prompted his kindness to a timid, lonely little girl whom he didn't really need to notice at all. Lorraine Griffiths lived in Yew Tree Cottage with her 'granpa' one of the gardeners under Mr McKinnon. Lorraine's story is that of a little child managing to survive hard times and hard work.

'Sometimes I'd go up through the woods and then down towards the castle to see if Granpa was ready to come from there and if he wasn't, sometimes Mr McKinnon would see me and if it was summer time he'd say 'go and pick the strawberries or a few apples' and he'd push me under the net for strawberries. And I'd stay in the garden then until my Granpa was ready. When he'd come out and find me there, he used to get annoyed and say that I mustn't come during his working hours. 'Come and meet me and sit on the top' he'd say. There used to be trees up there all fallen down and you could sit on them and have a squirrel perhaps by the side of you.'

In 1924 little Lorraine had gone to live with the Godels for reasons of her poor health and also to help out because Mrs Godel was often ill and Mr Godel was working at the Castle. Lorraine had already had a sad life. She had been in hospital with diphtheria and was only five when her mother died. For a while the family of six little children in Aberfan had had a bad time of it, being looked after by indifferent carers so that their father could go to work and earn money to keep them. After he remarried, Lorraine's new step mother took her to the doctor because she had eczema on her scalp.

'It was he *(the doctor)* who suggested I should go to live in the country. It was the best thing that ever happened to me, I never looked back. She took me with my belongings on the train to Machen Station as a little child of about 6 or 7 to stay with Mrs Godel who was *her* relation not my father's, although afterwards I always called them Gran and Granpa. I was wearing the hobnailed boot that a kind lady in Aberfan had given me when she had seen me barefoot in the street. The boots now rubbed on my legs and the blood ran into them. That annoyed my grandmother so she took them off and bathed my legs and put stuff on and the boots were put on the back of the fire and I never saw them again

In the foreground is the stream. No longer there is the little bridge over which Lorraine had to carry the water up to the house.

My step mother left me there and went home. I was very lonely on my own. I had eczema so bad in the head and coming from a house with four sisters and a brother, to one where there was nobody, was a very frightening experience for any child. In bed that night I had a very good cry. My Gran came upstairs and gave me the finest hiding I'd ever had in my life. I never cried again. But although my brothers and sisters had stayed with my father and stepmother, I didn't think at all that my family didn't want me.

I had to work hard to pay the Godels back for what they were doing for me: cooking and cleaning, helping Granpa in the garden and fetching water from the well. He had dug this well out himself on the Coed Ruperra side of the stream at the bottom of the garden and I used to have to carry quite heavy buckets across the little wooden bridge he had made.

If my Gran was ill I used to have to go the doctor's, to Dr. Briggs in Caerphilly, all the way over the mountain *(Rudry)*, get the medicine and walk all the way back. There was no money for bus fares in those days. And I wouldn't see a soul all the way.

Frank Godel working as a gardener at the castle would have had lots of garden produce to bring home, so there is no reason why Lorraine should have always considered that they were so very poor. Like others, he had a second job stoking the boiler for the heating in the castle and his son Walter remembered going with him to do this, picking mushrooms on the way.

Mary Thomas' family, at Cwm Leyshon and the nearest neighbours of the Godels at Yew Tree cottage thought that Mr Godel was kindly but quite poor. Mary said, 'He called my father 'Dad' although he was older than him! They were lovely neighbours. He didn't earn much money. I never saw any meat in their meals only vegetables.'

Frank Godel with his gramophone

It is possible that he hid his money in the garden as Lorraine mentions below and was careful how he spent it. – keeping it for his wife's illness perhaps.

'I was never given any money but still I was kept and I had clothes and everything but I didn't have pocket money unless I was going somewhere. Occasionally if I'd ask for money for sweets, Granpa would first say no and then 'Hang on, gel, I'll see.' And then he'd come back up in the house eventually with a couple of coppers in his hands and they'd be all covered in dirt because he used to hide his money. You'd never know where he hid it and you'd never see him going for it.'

Lorraine didn't go to school until she was ten when the 'school bobby' asked questions. Then she left when she was 14. She always thought she must have been dull because she couldn't read and write like the other children. Miss Jenkins in Rudry School was really kind to her and gave her extra attention. 'For reading you'd go in a little room. Miss Jenkins used to teach me to read. And encourage me a bit.'

Then when I left school I did a couple of hours' job with Mrs Miller in the Draethen. I used to scrub her house which was bare boards upstairs and bare flag stones down stairs and a long stone path to the toilet. Scrub all that on my hands and knees for half a crown a week and think I was very lucky. You'd have a dinner, but it wouldn't be a dinner like *we'd* cook. I'd have to polish her dresser with beeswax and then with oil for the other furniture. That would be a day's work from 9 30 till 5. Then I'd come home and if my Gran perhaps hadn't been well enough to cook, I'd have to cook the tea and probably if there was no water in the pan, go down the well and fetch it. One day my Gran said 'you're not going to Mrs Miller's no more to work for that money.' But then I had to work in her house instead. I worked until I got married and then I still had to look after her! But she was good to me when I had my first son. She used to look after him and nurse him.

Lorraine is on the right with her brother and step mother.

In the end, Granpa Godel's mind went a bit. There was nobody there to take him in to hospital, only me, aged about 15 then, but I went across to Cwm Leyshon Quarry to ask the manager there if he would drive my Granpa to the Royal Gwent. And I had to hold him in my arms until we got to the hospital because he didn't know where he was. He died very soon after. Mary and Enid Thomas's father was good to us then.'

After Granpa Godel's death Mrs Godel and Lorraine moved to Machen. Here she is seen on the right of the photo, with her first baby, her eldest brother and her step mother who had first brought her to Yew Tree Cottage. After bringing up her own family, she married for a second time and had a happy life in the end. She died in 2001. She was a cheerful soul.

CHAPTER EIGHT COED CRAIG RUPERRA THE ANCIENT WOODLAND

Little Lorraine, sitting on a log in Coed Craig Ruperra and watching a squirrel while waiting for her 'granpa', could not have been aware that the landscape around her was the consequence of thousands of years of man's impact.

Coed Craig Ruperra was probably cleared of trees on a regular basis. In Iron Age times a cleared site would emphasise the significance of the fort on the top, while the timber itself was a valuable resource both as a building material and for fuel for heating and cooking. It was an obvious focus for farming settlements. Later the Normans would have cleared the trees to have a good view of the terrain around their wooden castle on the mound.

By the Middle Ages woods generally were being carefully managed by the local landowning families for the sport of hunting, while special servants were used to kill the animals needed for food. We must presume that the Welsh owners of Ruperra, the descendants of Ifor Hael at Cleppa Park did the same. Gradually drastic laws were drawn up to prevent ordinary folk poaching the landowners' animals while rabbits introduced by the Normans for food – there are rabbit warrens near Coed Craig Ruperra on Machen Mountain – eventually became the poor man's supplement to his rations.

Thomas Morgan a younger son of one of the Morgans of Machen married into the wealthy Lewis family of Ruperra in the 16th century, thus acquiring the Ruperra Estate and building Ruperra Castle on the site of the medieval house there. From then until the estate was sold in 1956, the Morgans used Coed Craig Ruperra for hunting and shooting as well as for commercial purposes and employed many woodsmen. From time to time they added landscape features according to the current fashion, especially to the part of the wood just to the north of the Castle, where even today the planting forms a backdrop to the once landscaped gardens of the castle

In 1600 Coed Craig Ruperra is mentioned in the first records of Ancient Woodlands, meaning that no alien species of trees had been introduced up to that time. This situation continued until the mid 19th to early 20th century when some fashionable exotic trees like Scots Pine, Cedar and Cyprus,

Rhododendron and Laurel were planted as part of new landscaping. Angus McKinnon, head gardener from 1894 to 1932 would have planted some of these and his team of gardeners and woodsmen would have maintained them.

The remains of the coppiced beechwood

To maximise the commercial benefits of the woodland, the Morgans used the timber trade to advantage. Indeed the fine beech trees, the remains of which can be seen to the north of the path along the ridge leading up to the mound, were regularly coppiced to provide charcoal for local iron works. Estate workers could use only dead wood for fuel.

In the 1920s the first of an ever increasing tide of conifer was planted in Coed Craig Ruperra. After the first World War the drive to replenish the stocks of wood used up in the war effort meant that many woodland owners felled and replaced their native trees with the fast growing and more lucrative conifers. On the board of the new Forestry Commission's Committee for Wales set up by the Forestry Act of 1919 was the Rt Hon. the Lord Tredegar and John I Storrar, later a Tredegar agent from 1938 to 1944.

The ice storm of 1915 had destroyed many large mature native trees as well at this time, but not all of Coed Craig Ruperra was subsequently cut down and there are still some remains of the broadleaf ancient forest in parts.

A photograph taken in the 1930s from the Draethen shows the extent of the clear felling. A photograph taken at the same time, of the gardens of the Castle, shows the background of half grown conifers on Coed Ruperra with the relicts of native broadleaf trees behind. The sale details for Ruperra in 1935 mentioned Spruce, Larch, Douglas Fir and Scotch Pine – there were 394 acres of woodland on the whole estate at this time. The marine blockade of Britain during World War II meant that stocks of wood for home use were greatly depleted, the half grown conifer plantations having to be cut down and used. After the war there was continued pressure therefore to plant more fast growing conifer.

Coed Craig Ruperra in the early 30s, felled and replanted. The Hollybush is in the foreground and the motte can be clearly seen in the background.

New conifers growing on the southern slopes of Coed Ruperra. The new glass house can be seen at the top of the steps.

But back at the end of the 19th century Coed Ruperra was still mainly ancient woodland. Joseph Spooner had started work on the estate as a young post boy whose job was to travel down to Lower Machen Post Office to pick up the mail. Colonel Freddie, as Member of Parliament for Monmouthshire received a lot of mail. Joe's grandson, Bernard Spooner recalls the gruesome tale of his grandfather and a beech tree.

'At that time my grandfather had either bought or been given a pocket watch and was timing himself to see how long he took to get from the castle to Lower Machen and back. There was a particular beech tree in the woods on the way where he would stop on each journey and look at his watch to check the time. At this time one of the butlers disappeared from the Castle. They were searching for him everywhere and couldn't find him. Three days later they found him hanging in the beech tree. My grandfather had never noticed him because he was so intent on looking at his watch!'

Doris Oram remembers that 'the woods were kept beautifully. You could walk on the lovely rides. They were like lawns, all grassed over. There was one going from Tresguthan, where there's a gate now, into the woods and over to the Castle. There were a lot of woodmen working in the woods keeping them all tidy and watching out for fires. We used to go over to Ruperra a lot when I was a little girl. My father worked on the estate. There were lovely views from there and the banks were full of snowdrops and then daffodils at different times of the year. It looks as though people have dug them out by the roots because they've all gone now.'

Roy Hawkins says 'There were woodsmen working in the woods all the time and if your family worked on the estate you could go anywhere you liked. If you were a stranger the woodsmen would send you packing! All the paths were beautifully kept and even if you went off the beaten track it was easy to walk between the trees. There were some huge oak and beech trees there.

Only on hunting days were outsiders allowed to go in the woods. Hunting and shooting played a big part in the lives of the Morgan family. The hunt was a big event and crowds of people would follow on foot every week. There were no restrictions for the huntsmen either. Lord Tredegar owned the whole estate and the hunt could

Outside the Hollybush 1900. Some of the workers who kept the rides clear

go anywhere. They hunted all over Craig Ruperra, steep though it was and the woods were kept in perfect condition.'

Eileen Woodward whose father was William Greenway, game keeper from 1905 to 1919, lived at Spout Cottage when she got married.

"We were honoured to be able to go into the estate when we liked because my husband worked there. We took the estate as though it belonged to us. We went wherever we wanted to. There was a little brook up in the wood by Spout cottage, and we used to go up there for picnics and have a whale of a time."

By 1920 a new summer house had been built on the mound and before the newly planted conifers had grown tall it could be seen for miles around, just like the Iron Age fort two thousand years before, and, for that matter, like it is today. Roy Hawkins remembers that

Agnes McKinnon and Robert at the entrance of the spiral path to the new summerhouse

'The views from the top of Craig Ruperra were breathtaking. There were no trees around the top. The mound was grassed over as were the steep banks below it. Even by the 1930s the trees lower down were only about five feet high. At the beginning of the path up to the summerhouse there was a little gate with a fence on the left hand side leading up to another little gate which let you in through the wall around the summerhouse. They were all painted white. The summerhouse was hexagon shaped with posts driven into the ground at each corner. Bench seats were attached round the split log walls. The roof was thatched and the floor cobbled. The whole place was delightful.'

Bert Stradling remembered that 'from the summerhouse on Craig Ruperra there was a lovely view especially of the Draethen. In the old days the houses in the Row in Draethen had their gardens on the opposite side of the road. This was before Cardiff Rural District Council built the houses there in the 50s. When the apple trees were in bloom it was a marvellous sight and you could see Machen Quarry behind it. The summerhouse had a roof and a big wall around it and a place inside to sit down. The Morgans had a table in there and used to go up there for picnics.'

Tommy Harris who has lived in Machen all his life remembers that 'the view from the summer house was fantastic - right across the Channel and all around. The path to the summer house came up from the Hollybush side, then you could wander down to the Castle on the other side. The summerhouse itself was a wooden building perfectly round and was very solidly built, well, everything on the Estate was solidly built. There was a seat inside, just a rough bench around the wall. The walls were made of trees cut in half so they were round on the outside and flat on the inside and butted together. There were cracks between them, they weren't solid, the draught would come through but it was ample protection from the rain or anything like that.'

Terry Everson, as a little Machen girl of eight or nine, mentioned walking over to Ruperra on a Sunday night in the late 30s. 'After we'd climbed up to the summerhouse we'd have chocolates and sweets. The summer house was intact in those days. It was conical with a thatched roof and wooden slatted seating all round from one end of the doorway to the other. There was no door just a doorway looking south and no windows. My father always said it was built for Lord Tredegar's sister to take her knitting, sewing and reading up there. But what a climb and not very good light for her! But there were beautiful views and from the doorway you'd be looking down over the Castle and beyond. Once you got up on the flat there was quite an area round the summerhouse where you could walk. It was very very steep to get up there. You used to be able to see it above the trees from a long way away.

We'd walk from Machen to Draethen through the Six o'clock Field. It used to be all open field and in the Spring carpeted with lovely primroses. It wasn't like it was later with all those fir trees there. Then we'd go up behind the Hollybush. The field there would be snow white with snowdrops in the early Spring. People used to come from miles around to see them. There'd always be lots of people walking around because of course there were no cars. And people socialised more when they were out.

On Easter weekends Ruperra was like a Mecca. We'd always go in a crowd as children and we'd walk over to Ruperra Castle after dinner on Easter Monday with our Easter eggs and a bottle of pop. There was no litter in those days. You didn't throw your pop bottles away. You brought them back to get a penny refund from Mrs Jones Top Shop! There'd be no end of people over there, walkers and cyclists. If we were lucky and there was enough room, we'd sit on the wall to eat our Easter eggs, otherwise we'd have to sit on the banking. Then we'd go high up on Craig Ruperra and there we would be looking down on the Castle! We'd have reached our goal!'

View of the castle from Craig Ruperra

Marion Beeston from Lower Machen remembers that particularly at Easter time, 'a special bus would bring people from Newport to enjoy Ruperra and its woods. There were so many people about in those days. And you could go for cups of tea and cake in the Draethen. Both Mrs Brittain and Mrs Lloyd served teas for 'tourists'! From Lower Machen you could see all the lovely primroses and bluebells growing in the fields and we children used to go and pick them. But it was not the picking that made the flowers disappear; it was the planting of conifers after the First World War that did for them'

The thickness of the mature conifers

Edna Merrett tells the story of her Godel grandparents at Yew Tree cottage, who, when 'strangers knocked at the door asking did they do tea and cakes, actually made some for them!' *She also learned the romantic tale of her father wooing her mother with a bunch of snowdrops from Yew Tree cottage.*

After the sale of the contents of the castle in 1935 a skeleton staff guarded the woods but could not possibly look after the paths and the rides. After the Second World War when the Morgans finally abandoned Ruperra, the condition of the woods slowly deteriorated, the dense conifers changing the ecology of the plant and animal life, which sank beneath the soil waiting like Sleeping Beauty for a Prince Charming to rescue it.

When the estate was sold in 1956, the woods became almost entirely a commercial plantation, with more conifers being planted. Now fifty years later, with the conifers felled, once again people can enjoy the wonderful views from the top. Furthermore because a few broadleaf trees were left standing on very

top by the previous owners, a distinctive straggly silhouette has been formed which can be identified quickly and effortlessly from all around the area, including the M4 motorway – but looking at it is not to be recommended if you are the driver! The clear felling however has brought its own problems. Now that the dense conifers have gone but the new trees are still very small, the site has been colonised by bramble and bracken which are proving very difficult to clear. These will gradually recede however, once the new trees grow.

As for the wild animals in the wood, there were always plenty of squirrels and rabbits. The rabbits were wiped out by myxomatosis in the 50s but they are beginning to come back now. No one mentioned in their recordings any cruel trapping of animals on the estate while the Morgans were in charge or after their time, although there was plenty of it described in the surrounding districts. Let's hope that wild animals can now live their lives in peace and in their own way in the whole area around Ruperra.

CHAPTER NINE HOUSEWORK IN THE CASTLE AND ESTATE.

Although the woods and the parkland were kept in good condition for sporting events and family pleasure parties, after the death of Colonel Freddie in 1909 and after Courtenay's taking up residence at Tredegar House in 1913 there were far fewer domestic staff in the castle. If the family from Tredegar House visited, they would usually bring their own staff with them and as we shall see, relations were not always cordial. However for the first two decades at least of the 20th century domestic staff were still being hired and fired.

In the census returns for the Castle and outbuildings in 1891 there had been nineteen servants living in. In the castle there was one butler, one footman, a laundry maid and a kitchen maid, two valets, two housemaids, three grooms and three ladies' maids, with another five in the outbuildings.

In 1901 there was a butler, a waiter, a footman, a groom, a cook, two lady's maids, two laundry maids, a dairymaid, three housemaids, a kitchen maid, a scullery maid, three stud grooms and a gamekeeper and his wife – again nineteen in all.

William Beechey gives us an insight into the domestic difficulties at the Castle which occurred from time to time. This particular problem had started in 1900.

'June 21st Mrs Jones the cook and the two kitchen girls left. The laundry maid left.
July 25th Advertising in the Western mail for a kitchen maid and a scullery maid. £16 and £10 (*per annum*)
August 7th the new cook came tonight. Mrs Jones and a new kitchen maid.
Sept 21 Mrs Jones the Cook gets drunk. She's got to go. No-one likes her. Tells lies. Bad thing.
Oct 19th Mrs Jones the old cook gone. Done no good. She was a woman they were all glad that she had left Ruperra.
November 13th The Cook gone again in a minute's notice.
1901 Feb 1st New kitchen maid to the castle today. Tom went to meet her 3 trains but did not see her.
Feb 2nd Miss Phillips the new cook left.

Feb 7th Miss Miller was up today about the lunch. She was in a terrible bad temper. She had Mr Rymer *(the bailiff)* up to her and had me on in the kitchen. Miss Phillips the job cook had only had 3 sheep in January. There is no good in these job cooks. They make bad for others and cooks.'

By the mid 1920s however the Castle was just ticking over, with the furniture covered in dustsheets, although right up until the early thirties, staff were still being taken on. Very often the living conditions for the servants at the Castle were far superior to those of the homes they came from, although those who lived in, often missed the rough and tumble of family life. Many local people of course walked to work. Mary Thomas was one of these.

'Before I went to Ruperra, when Colonel Morgan lived there, there was a full staff, butler, footman and all. Edwin Jones *(Kath Ayres' father)* worked the electric generator in the power house. He was going out with a laundry maid. Auntie Louie from the Griffin was a parlour maid in the Castle. Aunty Mary the Mill was from away but working in the Dairy and Gladys Perkins' mother was the head dairy maid. When I started in the Bothy in 1920 I was getting £3 12 a month. In 1928 Lord Tredegar spent half a million on Ruperra getting it right for his son Evan who was getting married.'

As we know, Evan never came to live there. Even the beautiful accommodation made for the chauffeurs in the Bothy was never used since they all stayed at Tredegar House. There were plenty of gardeners however. Mary remembered eight young gardeners sleeping there and they had a great big day room as well.

'The boys were only having 16 shillings a week. *(Which is only eight shillings less than Mary herself, but it would have made a big difference in those days.)* On a Friday, Tom Pembridge would go to town to do the shopping for everybody. You could buy a joint of lamb for about two shillings. The boys would have their joint and fresh veg from the garden. They'd be eating well because they were working out in the fresh air. I used to make a spotted dick for them, with suet and brown sugar and big raisins and boil it in a big cloth and make a big basin of custard. Well they'd eat that until they'd take the grease off the plate. I used to make a pie and Mr Blackburn the head keeper down the bottom of the Park, would say 'Good God Mary whatever have you got cooking here, it's beautiful!' And it would only be potatoes, sliced, and onions and maybe Mrs McKinnon would have given me something to put in it, but that's all they'd have for a couple of days. Once that meat had gone they couldn't afford any more. I used to stuff a marrow for them. They'd have the place at the Bothy for nothing and all the vegetables from the garden but anything else they paid for out of their wages. I had an hour for my dinner. I used to take sandwiches from home for my lunch everyday and then I'd have a cooked meal when I got home

When I was working in the Bothy, I made lots of jam for the boys with all the fruit of the garden. The saucepan was huge and heavy before you put anything in it! I had to pick it up off the fire full of boiling jam boiling over. It frightened me to death. But the boys were so pleased with that jam. One of the boys used to see that the fire kept in over night. I had to tell Mr McKinnon about one of them who wasn't seeing to the fire properly.

Mary sitting by the steps to the glasshouse.

I used to have to go over to the castle to change the beds. And bring the bed linen over to the Bothy to be washed. I worked in the Castle when Lord Tredegar came up for a shooting party, washing up all day for 4 shillings and 8 pence and the saucepans had to be perfect. Your hands got very bad. Cuts right down in the sides of your fingers. Lemon and glycerine we used to put on them. You couldn't grumble about anything. And to ask for a day off was like asking for the moon! But at the time I was quite happy, I was happier than many. Of course I thought I was very rich. I can't remember being tired - of course we were young, but we must have been tired. And you had to do things thoroughly; Mrs McKinnon wouldn't have anything half done. You had to get in the 'corrners' as she used to say.

I went up to the Council in Ystrad Mynach some time ago for a medical and the Doctor said 'You're remarkable for your age. Have you been pretty active in your life?' We all had to work hard. There weren't all the machines like today. You had to do something very bad to lose your job. It was easy for the men to get drunk, mind, because they were brewing their own beer there. It was good stuff when whisky was 3/6 a bottle. One day when a man was drunk on this beer, the others shaved off half his beard, half his hair and half his whiskers!'

Another servant Mrs Penhaloric was born in 1909 in Bedwas and died there in 2001. At the age of seventeen in 1926 she got a job at Ruperra Castle and eventually became the cook.

'On my days off (one day a week) I used to walk home and then back to Ruperra Castle, either from Rudry or from Lower Machen because the buses weren't like they are today. You'd only have one now and again. My father used to come to meet me when I was walking home. It was a long walk.

I enjoyed it there, I enjoyed the job. There were four of us in the Castle looking after it and we girls shared a nice bedroom. There was the housekeeper, two housemaids and myself. I cooked for the four of us. The food was home grown. Dear me, those were the days! Your life wasn't your own. We'd get up about 6.30 in the morning and we'd finish about 9 at night. And we were on all the time. I was in the kitchen all the time. I started as a scullery maid and Mrs McKinnon did the cooking then. The other two maids kept the place tidy. There wasn't much to do with no one living there but it had to be done. Whether it was clean or no, they had to go over the same thing all the time. It wouldn't do for them to shirk it. She'd be watching them. She'd have her rod out! I never got into trouble though.

I liked the surroundings and from my kitchen window I could look right across the channel so it was pleasant but not like being home. I missed my family. But being one of seven in those days you had to get out, you didn't have any choice. And my father wasn't well so he wasn't working very often. He was a miner. He had emphysema. Once I got to fourteen and could leave school, I had to go.

The gardeners would bring all the vegetables for the cooking and the meat would come off the estate - a lot of poultry and rabbits. There was plenty of food. We'd have meat every day. They didn't stint. We were well looked after. Once or twice the staff from Tredegar House came. They didn't like it; it was too quiet for them. The Butler and two footmen would come if the family were coming, the preparation was tremendous. You'd think royalty was coming!

Lord and Lady Tredegar used to come sometimes but *she* didn't like it. She was a London girl. It was too quiet for her. We'd have a message to say that we had to have everything prepared and ready for them. They'd come in the morning but they'd pack up and go in the afternoon. Couldn't stick it. I suppose in London they'd have all the life and that. They would come to Ruperra when they were staying at Tredegar House from London.

There was always somebody or another there shooting and the gardeners and some little boys used to go out beating the pheasants for them to kill. I've feathered enough pheasants to last a lifetime. Perhaps after a day's shooting there'd be as much as thirty pheasants left for me to deal with. They'd be hung up in the kitchen. I've seen them when they were hanging up, moving with maggots. Horrible. Horrible. They had to be ripe before we could feather them. It wasn't a very nice job but like everything else you'd get used to it. I tasted them once or twice but I wasn't very fussy on it. I was never one to go for it. They'd leave them hang too long for me.

The pay wasn't very good. It was good for those days I suppose but I never saw much of it because I used to take it home for my mother. As I was the eldest and there were a few of us, it helped. It didn't do me any harm. I'd feel hard done by sometimes when I'd see the others going out dancing and that but I never had the chance. I had to be home to be there with my mother.

Mary Penhaloric aged 90

I hadn't met my husband then. He was a big friend of my brother's and used to visit my house. That's how I met him. He was a gardener at Ruperra and from Cornwall. I think I fell for his looks! He was a good looking man. A very kind man. We were married twenty odd years. He was a miner so he didn't have to go to the war. He died when he was 40 odd, very young. My world fell apart when he died. I had 6 children and I've still got them. They've never given me any worry. I've got fourteen grandchildren and great grandchildren. It's quite a handful when they're all here. I don't get out much now. I think I'm getting lazy! I have worked hard all my life.'

When Mrs Penhaloric recorded this she was over 90 years of age. After leaving Ruperra, she had worked in the Council Offices in Caerphilly and used to bring in cakes she had made herself for the office staff. A very kind lady.

Jenny Preece went to work as a maid in Ruperra Castle when she was sixteen in the 1920s. She wanted the job because she had fallen in love with a young gardener there but she soon lived to regret it! 'I had met my gardener at a little dance on a Saturday night at the Church Hall in Rudry. Our vicar Mr Raymond knew we were friendly. I had a chat with him because you could tell him anything. I told him that I'd had words with my father because he'd said I was too young to have boyfriends and I said 'I'd like to get to work, Mr Raymond and I know they want staff at Ruperra Castle. He said, 'I know Miss Watts, would you like me to put a word in for you, but you must speak to your Mam and Dad first.'

Jenny Preece 1995

I got the job but I detested it from the first day I went there! The Castle was like a fortress and Miss Watts was so prim and proper! What can I say! You had to buy your own uniform, which my mother and father did, fair play to them. They didn't want me to go but they said to give it a try and if I liked it, to stay. I didn't think about the pay! I just wanted to get there so that I could see my boyfriend passing by the window! When I look back on it now I think 'What fools we are at 16!'

Four of us maids shared a bedroom. There was lovely furniture in it but it was right at the top of the building and there were some stairs to get to it I can tell you! By the time you got to the top you were ready to lie down never mind sit down. You were well fed, you had clean beds and were not ill-treated in any way. You were severely scolded if you hadn't done what you were supposed to do but apart from that we were better off than if we had stayed at home.

Furniture covered in dust sheets.

There wasn't a terrible lot of work because everything was covered in dustsheets but it was a tremendous place and we still had to keep all the furnishings immaculate. The front hall was very elegant. If you looked up you could see the stair right to the top as if it was suspended in mid air, not a pillar holding it. There were pictures of Lord Tredegar's ancestors on the walls.

Downstairs underground there was the kitchen. That was enormous! The ovens were in the middle of the room so you had to walk all the way around them All the pots and pans were hanging on the wall and it all looked very impressive, there's no doubt about that!

The suit of armour on one of staircase landings.

Then suddenly there would be a rush - 'His Lordship is coming tomorrow with a little party.' Then all the dust sheets would come off all through the place. The grates were enormous with great big stands, which had to be done with emery paper - that was the most horrible job ever! All the figures in the grates and the armour on each little landing had to be kept without a speck of dust on them, even in the cracks.

When Lord Tredegar had been shooting, pheasants would be hung up in the kitchen until they stank. The place used to be stinking of pheasants. How the cooks managed, I'll never know. I had to help with the feathering and I used to cry because the maggots would be climbing up over my hands.

There was a staff dining room, the servants' hall, very big with a huge table down the middle. When there was any big do the staff would come from Tredegar House and you sat in order of status. Of course I was at the bottom end of the table, wasn't I! When Lord Tredegar came he brought a butler, 2 footmen and about 20 staff with him. Perhaps he'd only stay one night and there'd be all this upheaval! When he wasn't in residence we were only four so we used the butler's pantry for our meals. Of course we had to clear out of there when the butler from Tredegar House came. He took over then with the kitchen maids and scullery maids and you had to be on your best behaviour. We were the underdogs. We were 'the Ruperra' we weren't 'the Tredegar House.' You had to shut your mouth and do as you were told. And believe it or not, if one of the Tredegar housemaids wanted something from their bedroom I was told to go up and get it. I was of the same status but it made no difference. They wanted to show their authority. One time after being sent all the way up those stairs two or three times for something trivial, I said 'If you want it from upstairs, fetch it yourself!' I was reported to Miss Watts and severely told off. By this time I didn't care because my gardener and I had finished anyway!'

In the early 1920s, May Jones from Llandyssul, on a visit to relatives in Castleton, went to church at Lower Machen with them. Tom Pembridge, her husband-to-be was sitting in Church. He was the chauffeur at the Castle. 'After

May and Tom on their motorbike

church we all went for a walk and I heard that they needed a maid at the castle. But generally you'd find out about where the jobs were from the men who used to go round selling seeds and pots and things.

There were only two maids at the Castle when I was there and five at Tredegar House. You had to buy your own uniform, a print dress for the morning and then a black dress with a white apron for the evening. Sometimes I'd have to go down to Tredegar House if they were very busy there. If the family were staying at Ruperra you had to get up at 6 am and clean the floors, especially the dining room, and light the fires, all very quietly before they got up. After that you didn't touch the fires. Frank Godel would bring the wood for the fires and see to them. He also saw to the boiler in the basement which heated the house. The Morgans made their own electricity with generators.

You'd have your breakfast in the Servants' Hall and then you had the afternoon mostly free. Then there'd be tea in the housemaids' room. There was always plenty of food and the kitchen staff washed up. If you heard any of the family coming when you were about your tasks, you'd keep out of the way. When they went into dinner in the evening, you'd clean the toilets and the baths and change the towels. They had clean towels every day. You'd turn the beds back as well. After dinner the guests would go to the smoking room. We'd be in bed by 9 pm since we were up at 6 am. The work wasn't too hard and you had one day off a week and then every other Sunday off. Tom and I were married in 1924. He was thirty three and I was twenty six.'

The story that now follows illustrates so well the difficulties that faced young children who took up a job at a stately home and had to fend for themselves, sometimes finding support from their colleagues and sometimes not. It also shows how an innocent child's life was affected by being illegitimate in those days. Born in Skenfrith in 1914, Gladys Phillips went into service when she was thirteen and a half. When she went to Ruperra a year or so later she was not a happy girl as her foster mother had died.

'I was born out of wedlock in 1914 and was brought up by an old lady and it was a secret. She was marvellous, she absolutely ruined me. On a Sunday she used to nurse me and sing hymns to me because she was very religious. She used to skim the cream off the milk and give me the cream. We always had best butter. I lived with the old lady right from a baby. I only knew my mother through village gossip. 'That's Nellie Vaughan's child, isn't she like her mother' So you keep it inside your head and ask no questions. One day the old lady said 'I must send these papers to your Auntie Nell' and when I asked why, she said 'She should be your best friend.' I said 'I know, it's my mother.' So she said 'Well, being it's you told me I can't deny it'. Because of course she had promised not to tell. So whenever I got in touch with my mother it was always as Auntie Nell. She knew I was being looked after and she never bothered with me at all when I was a girl. The old lady was eighty one when she died and I was only fourteen. She died years before my own mother. As I got older she had suggested that I went to a lady in the village who took young girls to train for domestic service. She said 'I'm not forcing you' but she wanted to see me on my own two feet before she died. So when she knew I was working she died happy.

Gladys Phillips aged 13 and a half

I started work at a place called Blackrock in Skenfrith when I was thirteen and a half. It was very nice there. It was what you'd call moderate work. We used to get up at six o'clock, open our windows, strip our beds, and make morning tea for the mistress. Then we'd have to go back and make our beds, open all the other windows and get the rooms ready. We'd go and empty the washbasins and all that and make the ladies' beds and tidy their rooms and then at a particular time we'd have to start what they called the 'work of the day' and that would be turning a room out completely. We had to finish that by lunch time and then change into our afternoon uniform. We had two hours off every afternoon and then at night we used to take hot water for them to wash for dinner because they had no basins and things in those days. We'd turn their beds down and draw the curtains, probably put out an evening dress for them. After twelve months when the lady thought we were fit to go she liked us to move on. I was supposed to be trained as a housemaid but I thought I'd go as a second housemaid as I didn't feel confident of going single.

So I went to Kinnersley Castle and it was a dreadful place, really wicked. It wasn't a real castle. It was built where a castle used to be. We were quite a lot of staff there - a lady's maid and two in the kitchen, and the butler and the parlour maid and two housemaids. Of course the butler was always head of the servants. He used to sit at the end of the table and keep an eye on all of us.

There was a lady there who used to go hunting. I used to have to put a fire in her bedroom and half the time the blessed thing wouldn't burn. I was only there three months when I got the sack. I knew the butler didn't like me because he was always going on about my dirty hands, although it was he who gave me all the dirty jobs, like getting the coal and carrying it to all the different rooms. I had to do all the fires, steel grates and white hearths, and all the steps round the castle. Cleaning the brass cans, scrubbing the back stairs, doing the maids bedrooms.

We worked till about 4 o'clock, then the butler would look at my hands because they were terrible with all the dirty jobs. One afternoon I was doing the back stairs and I was tired and instead of washing the soap off with water, I just wiped the soap off and he told me I was a silly fool. So I said, 'He that calleth his brother a fool shall be in danger of hellfire.' So he reported me for being cheeky and of course I got the sack.

Well after that I went to the Registry Office to get a job, since in those days I think they kept your references there. They gave me Ruperra and I fancied it. Perhaps they didn't know at Ruperra that I'd lost my job at Kinnersley. I was fifteen and a half when I went to Ruperra. It must have been about 1930. There was only a housekeeper, a housemaid, myself and Queenie, who became my friend. I think Queenie did the cooking and we lived up in the Butler's pantry mostly on boiled beef and carrots! It was quite nice, mind you, but I don't remember us having a lovely roast dinner like roast lamb and things. I don't remember how much pay we had but most of the places used to give you your uniform as well. I had to take mine to Ruperra.

I used to have to look after the housekeeper as if she was a lady, which I resented because I thought I was going to work for Lord Tredegar! You'd have to make her fire up and everything. I never had much to do with her and I suppose she gave the orders to the housemaid who passed them on. I knew I had to get my polish after breakfast, go round every room, polish, polish, polish and rub it in, on my knees, until you couldn't see a bit of polish. Then the housemaid used to go over it with a little polisher. Then you had your lunch and you went on again until 4 o'clock. This happened everyday because it was supposed to be a show place. It's a wonder I didn't have housemaid's knee.

The Banqueting Room

Lord Tredegar came once but I never saw him He'd been in his study apparently and had left his cigarette or cigar, so they said his lordship had been in there. Whenever he came he brought his staff from Tredegar House. Of course nobody ever came to stay in Ruperra. It would have been lovely if they had. There would have been parties and everything. There was nothing at all. Just slavery. I should think the reason was that they were getting ready to sell but we weren't told till the last minute.

On our one half day off a week, we'd get away just after lunch, walk to Church Road Station in Lower Machen or get a bus to Newport. I used to go to my aunt's at Newport on my day off. It took about half an hour to walk to Church Road. The last bus used to get us back before 10 o'clock. Not many girls would walk through the trees in the wood on their own in the night, so somebody from the farm used to come and meet us off the last bus. It was a straight walk through the woods. The first time I went, one of the farm hands said 'I've come to meet you off the bus' which I thought was strange at the time but he came once or twice.

I remember Queenie well because we shared a room. The gardener boys invited her round to the Bothy one evening and got her absolutely drunk on home made wine and she was ill all night long. They thought they were going to get me on it but they didn't! I'd like to know what happened to Queenie. I'm sure she lived locally. I'd like to meet Queenie again - Queenie Aust.'

Queenie was the same age as Gladys but in 1931 when Gladys had been at Ruperra for only three months, it was prepared for sale and the staff were dismissed and she and Queenie lost touch.

'When I went home after Ruperra that was the only time my mother was sympathetic towards me. She allowed me to stay home with her for about a month because I was so run down but she still didn't class me as a daughter. I told her I knew that she had worked for my father who was a drunken old man with a sick wife and that he had promised to marry her but had taken advantage of her. Eventually my mother left him and married a police sergeant and had six children.

In the end not one of her children wanted my mother and they were going to put her in a home. But my husband said it wouldn't be right and he allowed her to come up and stay with us. I know the old lady would have said 'You do it Gladys, it's your mother.' So she had the next room here downstairs, with her bed in it. I even prepared her for her last journey. I've got five children of my own and they are all good to me.'

CHAPTER TEN IMPRESSIONS OF THE CASTLE

The new east entrance porch to the castle.

How striking is the change in Ruperra's fortunes as described by Gladys Vaughan in 1931 when compared with the first decade of the 20th Century. Although Colonel Freddie Morgan was not inclined to spend much money on Ruperra he even so liked the peace and quiet there after the hustle and bustle of his life. It was said that his favourite sitting room was the north east corner of the ground floor. As his brother Godfrey didn't have any children it was expected that Freddie would succeed him as Lord Tredegar but Freddie died unexpectedly in 1909, four years before Godfrey. Lord-in-waiting was Courtenay Morgan, Freddie's son. When he inherited and went to live at Tredegar House, he continued the programme of new works at Ruperra that he had started. He had been brought up at Ruperra and loved and respected his childhood home, wanting life to carry on as before. He was unable to recognize the signs of impending disaster that faced the great country estates after the First World War. Instead of introducing improvements and innovations in agriculture to make the whole of the Tredegar Estates more efficient, he lived a luxurious life, hunting and shooting and sailing his yacht. In 1920 the Tredegar Estate actually bought up new farms. He spent, some locals say £1/2 million and others £3 million, doing up Ruperra for his son Evan who was about to get married. When he died in 1934 leaving £2,200,000 with death duties of 30%, the first place the trustees of the estates thought of selling was Ruperra.

Building the new stable block

In the first decade of the 20th century however, all was activity at Ruperra. Courtenay's programme of refurbishment included a new power house fitted with duplicate steam-driven generators, dynamos and boilers, a new reservoir and pump house in the deer park and a new east entrance porch to the castle.

Here are drawings by an unknown architect of the stable block first built in 1790 and although destroyed by fire in 1889, restored in the same style with the addition of the clock tower in 1905

The new Stable Block 1905

The brew house, laundry and dairy range (otherwise known as the Bothy) built in the 1840s, were now converted to accommodate the valets, footmen, chauffeurs and garden staff. The entrance to the Bothy is in the form of an arched doorway which leads to a roomy hallway with separate doors into each part of the house.

The refurbished Bothy with Angus McKinnon's chickens in the foreground.

Mary and Enid Thomas remember painters and decorators at work at Ruperra in the early 20s. Some of them stayed in the Bothy. 'There were Londoners putting in mosaic floors and no doors squeaked! A lot of cabinet makers and French polishers and people working on the greenhouses.'

In 1913 one of the most reputed firms of glasshouse designers in the country, Mackenzie and Montcur Ltd. were employed to construct the beautiful glasshouse that makes such a sad picture today. This firm had also designed glasshouses in Kew Gardens and the great Sefton Park Palm House in Liverpool, restored in 2000 with a Lottery grant. Although some people, perhaps wishing to justify its demolition, have recently described the woodwork of the Ruperra glasshouse today as 'terribly rotten', the teak is

The Grade II listed Glasshouse. On either end are the carnation houses.

hard and strong and the fish scale panes, although smashed and broken, still demonstrate what the structure must have looked like when Angus McKinnon knew it. The rusted water pipes, heating and ventilation structures still bear witness to its sophistication.

Colin Anstey who farmed the Home Farm after the Beecheys in the 30s thought it was possible that 'in the early 20's there had been money coming in from the 'golden mile', that is from the taxes that were levied on every ton of coal passing over Tredegar land on its way from the Valleys to the docks at Cardiff, Barry and Newport. No end of money was spent on Home Farm as well as on the Castle. A piggery like you've never seen before! It was like a palace!

A newspaper report of the wedding in the 1920s of Mr Rodney Forestier-Walker and Miss Mollie Vincent Clifford Wing at Michaelstone y Fedw Church, mentions that Viscount Tredegar had loaned Ruperra Castle for the reception. 'Masses of lilies, azaleas and hydrangeas lined the silver grey staircase of Ruperra Castle. The oak panelled banqueting hall was laid out as a buffet, with pink and red carnations as the decoration.' *Angus McKinnon must have supplied the flowers from the carnation houses on either side of the new glasshouse. I wonder did Mary Thomas help with the washing up.*

Gladys Vaughan knew of 'twenty three bedrooms in the house, which, being locked, I never saw. I recall the stately rooms more, with all this beautiful furniture, gold and red, and a balcony over the dining room. Down below there was a massive kitchen with a stone floor and a huge range.'

As a child Mary Thomas had made a special visit to the castle. 'On St David's day, children would go over to the Castle with a permit from Sir Foster Stedman. I remember walking around the top of the castle with the housekeeper. This was when the family was still at the castle. Ruperra was much before Tredegar House. Tredegar House is dark. At Ruperra you could sit in the window seats and look out over the Channel. Today it would be a marvellous home for old people. The housekeeper told us it took an hour and a half to open the windows, every morning and every night. The prophecy was that if it was burnt down for the third time it would never be restored. The front staircase was beautiful, made of wrought iron and painted a delicate blue and grey. The steps were marble. The rooms in the towers were round.'

Kath Ayres could remember going to visit Miss Watts, the housekeeper in the castle. Miss Watts had obviously progressed from the housemaid mentioned in the 1891 census. 'As a child, since I had family working at the Castle, I was allowed to go inside Sometimes she'd ask you in to her rooms for a cup of tea and biscuits. We'd go in through the back *(west)* door and up the staircase. It was a huge stairs and there were stone floors. And we were fascinated because she'd take us up into her room to see her Pekinese. If she didn't give him a saucer of tea and some biscuits he'd cry real tears and he'd be sat in his chair and the tears would be rolling down his face. We'd think that was funny! We thought it was all fascinating and we'd sit there and talk to her like old women!'

Winifred Ackland remembered her first approach to 'the two massive doors of the Castle but I never went inside. The hugeness of the doors made a great impression on me. I can remember thinking I'd never been anywhere near a big place like this before. There was no National Trust for us then!'

Bert Stradling remembered the deer in the park (to the west of the castle.) 'There was an avenue of oaks in that field. The Colonel was a terror for oaks. If one fell down he'd replace it immediately. There were longhaired Scotch cattle there and a flock of black sheep. The wool from the sheep was taken to a flannel mill and made into brown cloth for the coats and britches of the grooms and the keepers. There were lovely deer and my brother used to work there feeding them. There were deer stables there and a pump house further over.'

The deer sheds in the Deer Park

Bert was impressed by the roof of the castle. ''There was some lead on those roofs! I don't know what happened to it after the fire. You could walk all round those battlements, then you'd go up over the roof and walk all the way around the chimneys and all the coping was lead. Marvellous place.'

In 1918, three months before the Armistice, a postcard of Ruperra Castle, a peaceful, rural, stately home of great attraction, had been sent to Private Arthur Beeston, Marion Beeston's uncle, serving in France, from his cousin who was visiting his family in Lower Machen.

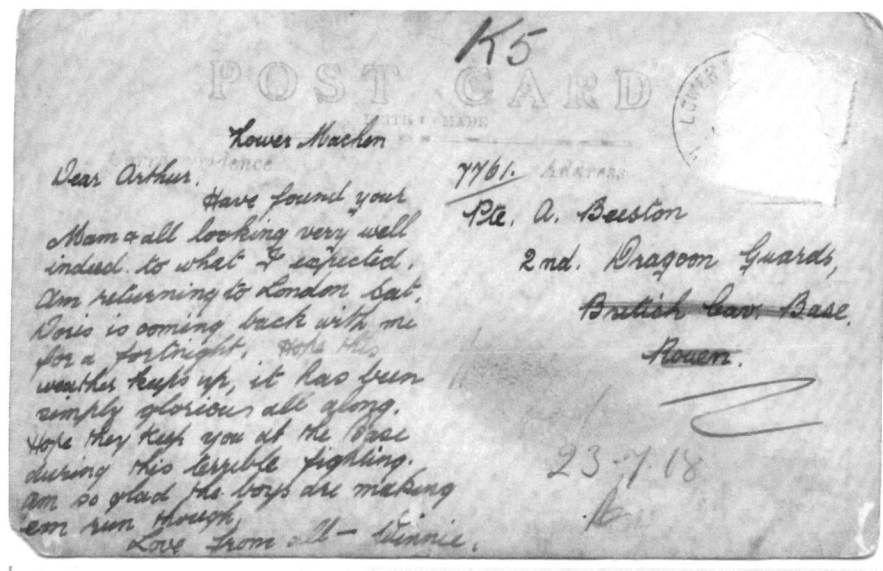

Later on, before the Second World War, Terry Everson and her friends from Machen could remember 'the nut trees on the right of the Castle wall. As you walked down the path alongside the Castle wall, you couldn't do more than *see* the nuts! They were well inside the high fencing, iron bars curved inwards with a mesh you couldn't get through!' *The girls didn't even try but Ron Gooding remembered going to the castle in the 30s* 'to try and get the nuts. There were filbut (*hazel*) nuts there, walnuts, chestnuts they had everything. There were apples in there as well. We were in our oils going over there of course.

Yet, after the death of Courtenay Morgan, the fortunes of the Tredegar Estates had declined so much that attempts were made to sell Ruperra. There were no offers. So in 1935 a sale of the entire contents of the Castle was held, a sale which is still talked about and in which many memorabilia and pieces of Ruperra furniture became the treasured possessions of local and not so local people. There are many people who have got something of Ruperra in their sitting room.

Mary Thomas spoke of 'eight weeks of sale at the castle and lots of things went, lots of clocks. Colonel Morgan would fancy a Grandfather clock in a tenant's farmhouse and the farmers were so silly, they'd give it to him. Things were going for a song. I bought a blue plate, a bird, a ginger jar and a big china bowl. They had Aladdin lamps during the sale so they must have shut down the electricity. There was cutlery in the Bothy that Mr McKinnon had never used. It went in the sale.

Terry Everson's mother and father went to the sale. 'My mother was entranced with the marble staircase! Late arriving, she was determined to have something! So my father had to carry home a cane basket chair with Chinese patterned upholstery from the Chinese Room in the Castle!'

By the outbreak of war in 1939 the castle and parklands had been virtually abandoned apart from a few trusted caretakers, and when the Castle itself was requisitioned for soldiers' billets in 1939, the first soldiers found it to be more or less empty apart from some chandeliers and some furniture in the Officers' Mess. Workmen were removing the last remains of glorious former times. The soldiers could see little bits of the wonderful marble staircase now boxed in with white timber that looked so out of place.

CHAPTER 11 THE END OF THE ESTATE

The wording of the advertisement for the sale of the Ruperra Estate with it's talk of golf courses, hunting and the best covert shooting in the County, showed that neither Courtney, Evan nor the Tredegar agents had grasped the truth of the economic situation of their agricultural holdings or of the country as a whole. The castle 'modernised in every particular' was now stated to be in 'first class order and condition.'

By Instructions from the Trustees of the Tredegar Settled Estates.

GLAMORGAN

The Historic, Agricultural and Sporting Estate

RUPERRA CASTLE

For Sale with **870** Acres
or **3,140** Acres.

Glorious Position facing South, 400 feet above Sea Level and commanding panoramic views of the Somerset Coast

Lying in a secluded position.

London, 2¾ hours (non-stop Express Train Service), Birmingham and the Midlands, 3 hours.

Two Golf 18-hole Courses in the immediate vicinity; Hunting with the Tredegar, Llangibby, Glamorgan and Pentyrch Foxhounds.

THE TITHE AND LAND TAX HAVE BEEN REDEEMED.

Evan moved in the same social and literary circles as the Duke of Windsor in those years between the wars. After his father's death in 1934 although he inherited about £10 million, Evan did not dedicate any of this to trying to rescue the fortunes of the agricultural estates, in serious financial trouble made worse by the death duties from 1909 and 1913. Evan died in 1949 and in 1956 the whole of the Tredegar Estates of 53,000 acres including Ruperra, with the castle now in ruins after the fire of 1941, was sold by his cousin John Morgan to the Eagle Star Insurance Company. Finally by 1962 with the death of John, the Morgan Family had died out.

Life for the former estate workers had become much more difficult. Mary and Enid Thomas found that the water supply to Cwm Leyshon Cottages, was stopped.

'We had had water in the garden until Evan stopped the water on us and then Tredegar sold the estate in the 1950s under those same conditions. Then we had to go as far as the Maenllwyd to get drinking water until the Council put a tap just inside our gate. It was a hard way of living. The Labour Councillor Mrs Dorothy Hearney wanted us to have the tap right outside the house but she got defeated in the next elections. We were very thankful to have it by the gate, but we never had water inside the house before we moved from there. When it froze we used to have to take kettles of boiling water to the tap. The big tank only held rain water; it was not for drinking. It would be better to drink out of the brook and boil it, than to drink standing water.'

The procedure of ringing up the Tredegar office to get repairs done had now ended. John Davies living in New Row, Machen, remembered Ruperra in the days when the estate was falling into decline. 'The estate workers had lived in their cottages around the estate rent free or for very low rent, but when the estate was sold, many had no money to buy them or do them up and so eventually they were condemned. One of them was in a terrible state when people were still living in it. You couldn't tell there was a house there!'

Some of the older estate workers were still kept on as caretakers as they had been in 1935, but there was no domestic or gardening staff. Tom Pembridge at West Lodge who had been a gardener and chauffeur in the 'good old days' was engaged to service the machinery. Game keeper Reg Blackburn continued to live at the Preserve and to protect the boundaries of the estate.

John Davies said that 'after the war I used to go round with Dai Spooner the pig butcher. Mr Brittain from the Draethen used to keep a pig for Doctor Davies in Machen. After the pig was killed, we'd hang it for a couple of days and take it from there in the Doctor's car to Ruperra Castle to be smoked. There was a little smoke house under the big wall behind the Stable Block by the kitchen greenhouse. It didn't have a very high roof and the pieces would be hung on hooks from the ceiling, just the one carcass at a time. There would be oak leaves put inside and once they were set fire to, the doors would be shut and the leaves would smoulder. Then you would have oak smoked bacon! There was no charge for this. There was no Lord Tredegar there then, just Tom Pembridge.

Keith Griffiths can remember being taken as a boy of ten, after the war to the Preserve at Ruperra. His uncle Tommy John Jenkins who lived at number five Upper Ochrwyth was interested in dogs and guns and was a friend of Reg Blackburn. Once a year, all the Jenkins family who lived in the thirteen houses at Upper Ochrwyth would get together, collect up the rhubarb, the mangles, and the earthenware jars and make rhubarb wine. They would make cider there too and Tommy John would take some of the Ochrwyth cider, with maybe bits from a pig killing to exchange for the Blackburn cider and so on.

An aerial view of Ruperra in the 1930s

The Jenkins family used to have wonderful 'get togethers' at Ochrwyth but as well as that they always held all their important family occasions at St Michael's Church at Lower Machen. So even after the Estate was sold, they stayed in close contact with all those people who had been at Ruperra all their lives.

It is part of human nature to look back on the pleasures of earlier days, even when there were great differentials. The family in the castle generated its own electricity and had running hot and cold water from the beginning of the century. Their standard of living was extremely luxurious compared even with the ones who lived in quite large estate houses. It took the passing of two world wars to change things. It is quite amazing to realise that although there was no electricity in Rudry until the 1950s and no running water inside some of the estate cottages until well after the Second World War, yet people still look back to the 'good old days'.

Living in the country around Ruperra today it is not very difficult to imagine what it was like when most people walked everywhere, and when only a few rode on horseback or in carriages. It is always a pleasant experience talking to old people who remember these times, but of course they are now becoming fewer. Yet when we write down their memories and later think about what they said, they are still with us. Bert Stradling considered the best time to go out was first thing in the morning when the air was clear and fresh. For him, being a countryman meant sitting quietly on a log in Ruperra, seeing little animals come out, and smelling the fragrant air of the meadows.

However this beautiful peaceful countryside is now at risk as big, new 'urbanised' houses spring up, sometimes so close together that they cannot nestle into their surroundings like the old ones did .As for the castle itself, how sad it is that we drive hundreds of miles to visit a stately home, when we have one of our own not five minutes away, falling further into ruin every day and no one seemingly able to do anything to save it.

When six year old Elwyn Edwards walked with his parents in 1935 over to Ruperra Castle from the Hollybush Inn, he noticed that it was a quiet walk because of the depth of the needles in the conifer wood, then alive with rabbits. He saw the Castle from the top and said 'Does a king live here? Because I couldn't get over it! Down on the paths not a weed, not a leaf out of place. Everything prim and proper, drives swept, wrought iron gates and marvellous lawns like bowling greens. Just inside the gates there were gravestones to dead pets.

After the War, another six year old, a girl, was also taken by her parents to see Ruperra Castle. She too reacted emotionally but in a very different way. She was so upset by the state of the castle and outbuildings that although she had never seen them before, burst into tears at the devastation.

In 1780 a Welsh bard, Evan Evans, curate at Bassaleg Church, visited Cleppa Park where lay the ruins of the court of Ifor Hael, the 14th century ancestor of the Morgans of Tredegar. He wrote a famous poem in Welsh, an 'englyn', regretting that the splendid hall where minstrels and bards had entertained was now just a heap of stones covered in brambles. Will the last line of the poem 'Mieri lle bu mawredd' which means 'brambles where once was greatness' describe the future of Ruperra? Will Ruperra gradually disappear into the earth with all its memories or will a new housing estate bury them?

The only remaining monuments to the existence of Ruperra may one day be the streets and houses, some of them public houses, named after it. And they are to be found often when least expected. As for the Morgans themselves – they may have left Ruperra, some might say they abandoned it, but their ancient family name dating back to the time of the old rulers of Wales, is preserved in the word Glamorgan. They could surely not want a better memorial.

Further Reading

Malcolm Airs, *The Buildings of Britain, Tudor and Jacobean*. Barrie and Jenkins 1982
Kathleen M. Burgess, *Frimley Park and Tekells Park Estates, a History*. Surrey Gardens Trust 2001
Cadw / Icomos *Register of Landscapes, Parks &Gardens of Special Historical Interest in Wales*. UK 1998
Caerphilly County Borough Council *Time Tracks Heritage Trail* 2001
Alexander Cresswell, *The Silent Houses of Britain*. Macdonald & Co 1991
G T Clark '*Limbus Patrum Morganiae et Glamorganiae*' 1886
Penny David, *A Garden Lost in Time*. Weidenfield and Nicholson 1999
Tony Friend. *Lord Tredegar's Ruperra Castle*. Community Design for Gwent. 1990
Mark Girouard, *Robert Smythson and the Elizabethen Country House*. Yale Univ. Press 1983
Cyril Hart, *British Trees in Colour*. Michael Joseph 1973
John B. Hilling, *The Historic Architecture of Wales*. Cardiff, 1976
Jeremy K. Knight. *Conflict and Community : Civil War and Popish Plot in Seventeenth Century Monmouthshire*. Logaston Press. 2005
William Linnard, *Welsh Woods and Forests, a History*. Gomer Press 2000
Thomas Lloyd, *The Lost Houses of Wales*. Save Britain's Heritage 1986
Benjamin Malkin, *The Scenery, Antiquities, and Biography of South Wales*. London 1804
Pat Moseley *Memories of Coed Craig Ruperra*. Ruperra Conservation Trust 1999
Ruperra Castle War and Flames. Ruperra Conservation Trust 2001
John Newman, *The Buildings of Wales, Glamorgan*. Penguin 1995
Roger Phillips, *Tredegar*. The Self Publishing Company 1990
Gwynedd O. Pierce, *Place-Names in Glamorgan*. Merton Priory press 2002
RCAHM (W) *Inventory of Ancient Monuments in Glamorgan Vol III Part Ia Early Castles*. HMSO 1981
RCAHM (W) *Inventory of Ancient Monuments in Glamorgan Vol.IV, Part I The Greater Houses*. HMSO 1981
Pamela A Sambrook, *The Country House Servant*. Sutton Publishing 1999
SAVE Britain's Heritage *Handbook* 1986
Simon Schama, *Landscape and Memory*. Fontana Press 1996
Tim Smit, *The Lost Gardens of Heligan*. Victor Gollanz 1997
Peter Smith, *Houses of the Welsh Countyside*. London 1975

Websites
www.ruperra.org.uk
www.members.fortunecity.com/tredegarhouse

How times have changed!

This is a very different picture to conjure up in our imaginations!

Margery Jones of Lower Machen, one hundred years old in April 2005, can remember the river Rhymney freezing up in the winter time. Local people used to skate on it and Marian Beeston's grandfather once skated as far as Machen from the bridge in Draethen. Marian remembers seeing an old pair of skates in the cupboard under the stairs and often wondered whose they were and when they were used. Fred Webb from the Draethen was a champion skater.!

Glossary of Welsh names.

Alltfarian   allt is a height or a cliff above a beach, marian (here farian) is a beach or a boundary.
Bassaleg   from 1. Bassilica, indicating the presence of a priory, or 2. maes-aleg, indicating Aleg's field
Cefn Mably   Mabli was the daughter of the Norman Fitzhamon. Cefn means ridge. It was a hunting lodge
Coed   wood
Craig/graig   rock
Cwm   valley
Cwrt y Cebydd   the court of the miser
Draethen   from traeth meaning beach and hen meaning old
Dyffryn   valley
Fedw in Michaelstone y Fedw   1. from bedw, a birch tree or 2. from St Medwy, a Welsh saint.
Ffald Gerrig   a stone fold
Ffwrwm Ishta   probably the lower furnace.
Garth   an enclosure or garden
Glan y Nant   On the banks of the stream.
Gwern   a swampy place of alders.
Leyshon   Welsh 'gleision' plural of glas (blue) but usually green when describing nature.
Llwyn Celyn   llwyn meaning a grove or bush and celyn, the holly
Machen   from 'ma' meaning place and chaen or chein the name of an early Welsh virgin saint. Hence Plas Machen , plas meaning a mansion, and Machen Fach meaning little.
Maenllwyd   maen is stone and llwyd, brown or grey
Minorca   perhaps someone had been on holiday there.
Ochrwyth   the left hand(chwyth) side (ochr) of the hill separating Machen from Risca
Rhiwderin   rhiw meaning hill or slope and derin from aderyn meaning bird
Rhyd y Gwern   Rhyd is a ford and gwern a swampy place.
Ruperra in Welsh Rhiw perrau,   rhiw meaning a hill or slope and perrau, pears.
Tawel   quiet or peaceful
Tresguthan   tre meaning the place of and sguthan a wood pigeon.
Ty   meaning house. Ty Gibbon and Ty Gowla are both the names of people who lived in the house.

Index

Photographs in bold italics.
Ackland Ethel 17, 23-25, 30.   *23 bottom W Knibbs*
Alltfarian 29.   *29 bottom*
Ansteys 59- 60, 109
Ayres, Kath 18-10, 27-8, 56-7, 61-2, 110.   *27 bottom* **(Marian Beeston)**
Beacon Alfred 26, 41, 60.
Beaufort Duke of, Henry Somerset, 11
Bedwas 56, 97
Beech Cottage 26
Beecheys 3, 25, 26, 29, 36-45, 52, 109. William 14, 25, 36-45, 94, Harry & Rowland 36, 44-5, Rosa 36-7, 44. Tom 25.   *36 top, 37-8, 45.* **(Elwyn Edwards)**
Beestons 28-9, 69, 92, 111.   *28 bottom, 29 centre, 111* **(Marian)**
Blackburns 26, 57, 60, 63, 95,114
Boer War 41
Bothy 23, 28, 34, 50, 54, 55, 68-75, 95-6, 105-8, 112
Brains Brewery 57
Brittain's 28, 92, 114
Butes 46, 55
Caerphilly 8, 9, 13, 18, 27, 30, 60, 83, 99, 117.
Cardiff 8, 15, 109, 117
Castleton 53 101
Cefn Mably 11, 46, 54, 57, 61.
Census Returns 36, 46, 47 - 51, 94
Charles I, Charles II 11
Church Road Station 47
Cliffords 25, 62
Coed Craig Ruperra (The woods) 3, 8, 42, 82, 86-93
Coronation Edward VII 43
Coslett Ivor 37, 63
Credgington 47
Crimean War 4, 16,
Cwm 31. Cwm Cottages 52
Cwm Leyshon 26, 34, 70, 113
Cwrt y Cebydd (Green Yard) 60
Davies John 114
Dineley 11
Draethen 26-29, 34, 46, 59, 61, 84, 87, 90-92, 114.
Eagle Star 8-9, 113.
East Lodge 17, 23, 25, 53, 63.
East entrance of castle.   *106 Edna Dix*
Edwards, Elwyn 3, 17, 23, 25, 53, 63 70.   *36 top, 37, 38, (taken by Miss Millar), 45.*
Edwards, Mrs, 30
Esther, Moses 38
Everson Terry 91, 102
Ffald Gerrig 31, 32, 34, 52, 53.
Forge The, 29
Friendly Fox (Garth) 22.
Gatehanger, Johnny 18

Godels 47,60, 82-85, 92, 101.   *84 Thomas family*
Gooding, Ron 102.
Graig View 29.
Greenway 17, 19, 62.   *19, Jeannie Wilson*
Griffin Inn 32
Griffiths, Lorraine 82-85.   *84 Raymond Johns*
Gwern y Goetre 29.
Gwernleyshon Farm 23, 38, 53.   *53 bottom Hywel Williams*
Harris, Tommy 56, 91.
Hawkins, Roy 34, 54, 88, 90.
Head, Walter 61
Heard W E 66.
Hearney, Councillor Dorothy 113
Hoare 40.
Holly House Farm 19, 62.
Hollybush 17, 22, 29, 46, 56, 61, 88, 91, 116.
Huthwaites 17, 26, 30. 38.   *17 G A James*
Ifor Hael 86, 116
Ironbridge 20, 26.   Ironbridge Cottage 25-6.
Jones Cissie 59.
Jones, Edwin 18-19, 61-2.
Lindsays 45, 56, 60.
Lisvane 30, 52.
Llewellyn Pearl (Oram) 32.   *33 left P.Llewellyn.*
Lloyd Mrs and Billy 28, 71, 92.
Llwyn Celyn 30.
Lower Machen 3, 23, 25, 28-9, 49,60, 66, 68, 71,73, 89, 92, 97, 101, 105, 111, 115.
Machen 17,34, 82, 86, 91, 112, 114.
Machen House 22, 37, 65, 74.   *22 Mike Ford*
Maenllwyd Inn 27, 113
Malkin Benjamin 12.
Mackenzie and Moncur 4, 108 – 9.
McKinnons. 3, 18, 21, 23, 34, 44, 46, 54, 55, 57, 62, 63, 64-81, 82, 87, 90, 96, 97, 108, 112. *64 top, 68, 69, 74, 76-81, 91 Ian McKinnon. 65 bottom, Iain Thornbear. 64 Surrey Gardens Trust. 65, Peter Kerr. 69 Tony Friend 74 108 D.Thomas*
Merrett, Edna 47, 60, 92.
Michaelstone (y Fedw) 3, 18, 26, 30, 38, 40, 46.
Millar Miss 43, 47(Census), 95   *38.*
Minorca Cottages 17, 29.
Molyneux 56
Morgans   Augustus (Rev.) 20, 37.
  (Sir) Charles Morgan Robinson 4, 20, 21.
  Courtenay (Lord Tredegar) 29, 41, 63, 75, 87, 104, 106-7, 109, 112, 113. Evan (Lord Tredegar) 4, 21, 63, 75, 95, 107, 113.
  Freddie (Colonel) 14, 17, 18, 21, 32, 36-40, 42-43, 55, 64, 89, 94 -5, 106. Frederick (Mr

and Mrs) 37. General (Morgan) 37. Godfrey (Lord Tredegar) 4, 16, 17, 20, 21, 30, 106. Jane (Morgan) and Charles (Gould) 21, 39. John (Lord Tredegar) 5, 113. (Sir) Thomas 12, 86, Tom Morgan 31-33.
Moriah Chapel Risca 20.
Mundy, Mr and Mrs 39, 55.
Newport 8, 12, 29, 42, 51, 59, 66. *9 Library.*
Ochrwyth 3, 60, 115.
Old Machen Station 56.
Oram, Doris 28, 46, 61, 89.
Park Wood 60
Parkfield House 23, 66, 71.
Parkwall (cottages) 31, 33, 34, 50 (Census) 70.
Pembridge 26, 46-47, 63, 95, 101, 114. *46, 101, D. Thomas*
Penhaloric Mrs, 97-99.
Penny, Sergeant, 26.
Philips Gladys 102-105. *103 Gladys Philips*
Philips John 18, 61.
Plas Machen and Machen Fach. 22,
Plymouth 46 59
Poachers 60-61
Post Office Lower Machen 18, 29, 89.
Powell Janey 55-6, 67-68.
Preece Jenny 99-101. *100 D. Thomas*
Preserve 19, 23, 55, 57–58, 114.
Price (Ironbridge) 23, 25, 26.
Price Dr William 23.
Primrose Cottage 61.
Public Bridleways and Footpaths 34, 54.
Queen Victoria, 4, 42.
Rae, Head Forester, 18, 46 61, 74.
Raymond (the Rev.) 99.
Reckless 26, 30, 41, 42.
Retreat The, 27.
Rhiwderin 60, 61.
Rhyd y Gwern Farm, 59.
Risca, 3, 20, 41.
Row, The, Draethen 27. *27 Marian Beeston*
Rowlands the Mill, 41
Rudry, 3, 17, 22, 23, 31, 33, 40, 47, 51, 56, 59, 61, 83, 84, 97, 99, 115.
Ruperra Castle. *Allan Nutt 9, 92 top.*
Ruperra Castle. 10 *Richard Kenward ABIPP 01873 890670 photo taken on behalf of the Building Conservation Directory.*
Ruperra Conservation Trust 8. *8 Rup. Cons. Trust.*
Ruperra Deer Park 37, 38, 42, 110. Castle Fire 8, 9, 63.
Ruperra Park Lodge 23, 24, 26, 27, 30, 33, 55
Ruperra Postcard 1930s *55 Dr Fred Holly*
Ruperra Sale, Estate & contents, 5, 93, 112, 113

Ruperra Stable Block 4, 26, 107. *107 top Thomas family. 107 centre National Museum of Wales. 107 bottom Jeannie Wilson*
Ruperra Summer House 90-91.
Rymer 38, 53, 95.
Spooners 18, 38, 40, 62, 89, 114
Spout Cottage 29.
Spring Jim, Herbie 3, 30, 37, 41, 63, 70.
Spring Cottage 30.
Squires Jack 47.
St Michael and All Angels Church 19, 20, 66, 74.
Stedman, Sir Foster, 22, 74, 109.
Storrar J D 22, 87.
Stradlings 4, 14, 17, 20, 26, 31, 32, 34, 43, 52, 54, 55, 58, 70, 90, 110,115. *52 Josette Hazel*
Stratton, Richard 16, 22, 40, 41.
Thomas Alfred MP 42-43.
Thomas Head Gamekeeper 26, 57-59.
Thomas Mary 17, 18, 34, 54, 68, 70-75, 95-97. *24, 25, 26 top, 32 53 top, 70 bottom, 71, 84 88 bottom, 96. Thomas Family*
Tirzah Chapel 20, 38-9, 45.
Tresguthan 29, 46, 61, 89
Ty Cornel 15, 31, 32, 35.
Ty Gawla 40.
Ty Gibbon 334.
Volland House 28-29
Yew Tree Cottage 27, 82-5
Watts Ted, 41, Miss Watts 99, 110
Webb, Fred,41. William and Mrs Mary, 18, 29.
West Lodge 23, 24, 26, 54.
Woodward, Eileen 97
World War I 14, 44, 45, 87, 92.
World War II 15, 63, 87, 93, 112, 115.

Servants on the cover picture of the book include

Mrs Lloyd, housekeeper at the Bothy (centre). Next to her probably Mrs Edwards, Reckless the gamekeeper's daughter married to the head groomsman. The little girl could be Mrs Edwards daughter.

Frank Godel, far right in the front row sitting on the ground

Also in the picture, Bert Edwards, Wheeler, Harry Beechey, Billy Lloyd, Ivor Coslett and Tiny Jones

The picture on the top of the book cover is taken from a picture postcard donated by Dr Fred Holly.